# HANDS-ON
# AMERICA
## VOLUME III

### ART ACTIVITIES ABOUT LEWIS & CLARK, PIONEERS, AND PLAINS INDIANS

This book is dedicated to my oldest daughter, Melinda Tietjen, her husband Allen and their family: Meredin and Steve Newcomb, Megan, Melanie, Jacob, and Eric. As a family, they have built an impressive log cabin in a sequestered canyon in central Utah — true to the tradition of their pioneer heritage.

Book design by Kinde Nebeker Design. Cynthia Oliver, as part of the design team gave the book its handsome appearance.

Laurel Casjens took the photographs.

Mary Simpson illustrated the book and assisted with the crafts.

Madlyn Tanner and Nancy Mathews edited and proofread the text.

©2009 Yvonne Young Merrill
First printing May 2009
Printed in China
All rights reserved

Library of Congress Control Number: 2001092322

ISBN 0-9778797-1-2
All rights reserved.

**Books by Yvonne Y. Merrill**

**KITS PUBLISHING**

2359 East Bryan Avenue
Salt Lake City, Utah 84108

info@hands-on.com
www.hands-on.com

**Hands-on Africa**
(ISBN 0-9643177-7-X)

**Hands-on Alaska**
(ISBN 0-9643177-3-7)

**Hands-on America Vol. I**
(ISBN 0-9643177-6-1)

**Hands-on America Vol. II**
(ISBN 0-9778797-0-4)

**Hands-on America Vol. III**
(ISBN 0-9778797-1-2)

**Hands-on Ancient People Vol. I**
(ISBN 0-9643177-8-8)

**Hands-on Ancient People Vol. II**
(ISBN 0-9643177-9-6)

**Hands-on Asia**
(ISBN 0-9643177-5-3)

**Hands-on Celebrations**
(ISBN 0-9643177-4-5)

**Hands-on Latin America**
(ISBN 0-9643177-1-0)

**Hands-on Rocky Mountains**
(ISBN 0-9643177-2-9)

# HANDS-ON AMERICA
## VOLUME III

## ART ACTIVITIES ABOUT LEWIS & CLARK, PIONEERS, AND PLAINS INDIANS

# YVONNE Y. MERRILL
## KITS PUBLISHING

Relics of the pioneer trek across the plains are rare and treasured. The objects in this picture of children's belongings feature a glimpse of a child's patchwork dress, sewn with thread carefully saved from unravelling canvas wagon covers.

Also shown are part of a wooden sock form for blocking handmade socks, a new shoe from a co-op store, a handmade crocheted ball, a toy spinning wheel, and a hand painted checkerboard.

*From the collection of*
*Daughters of Utah Pioneers Museum.*

# Table of Contents

# LEWIS & CLARK

## LOUISIANNA PURCHASE

Thomas Jefferson, third President of the United States of America, bought Louisiana from France in 1803 for $15,000,000. It added 825,000 miles to the country's size and amounted to 4 cents an acre. U.S. boundaries were now extended from the Misssippi River to the Rocky Mountains. Accordiing to the agreement, the USA held all the lands watered by the tributaries of the Missouri River. Jefferson had been interested in exploring the West—now he felt justified. Congress allocated $2,500 for the expedition. The goals were to look for the fabled Northwest Passage trade route and a quest for knowledge of plants, animals, birds,geography,and native cultures.

## THE LEADERS

Merriweather Lewis, 29, was chosen as captain of the Corps of Discovery. He chose William Clark, 34, as his co-captain. Lewis traveled from Pittsburgh to St. Louis seeking single young men who were "stout, healthy, accustomed to the woods and bearing bodily fatigue in a considerable degree." They ended up with 40 men, a Newfoundland dog, Clark's servant York, and several French guides. Lewis got a crash course in medical skills, botany and preserving plants, zoology, minerology, Indian history, astronomy, and fossils. Dr. Benjamin Rush assembled a fine medicine kit which included his own brand of laxatives the corps called "Thunderbolts." George Drouillard was hired as an Indian interpreter. The men trained at Fort Wood on the Missouri River from December 1803 to May 1804.

## GIFTS

Several tons of gifts were packed in waterproof containers: buttons, vermillion paint, ruffled shirts, knives with red handles, sulfur-tipped matches, ribbon, tomahawks, fabric, thread and needles, mirrors, tobacco and, of course, the silver peace medals—necklaces that are three inches in diameter and prized as gifts by Indian leaders.

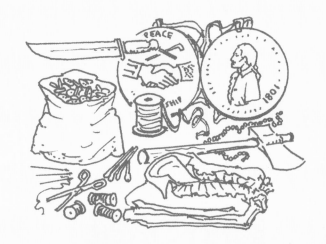

The Corps had excellent relations with the Indian groups they met. The Arikara had been decimated by smallpox. They were especially interested in York, the African-American. The Corps also met the Oto, Missouri, Osage, Assiniboine, and Wichita tribes.

## THE SIOUX

In August of 1804 the corps met their first Sioux. They had been warned of their crafty nature. There were three Big Sioux Nations east of the Missouri: the Dakota, Nakota and Lakota. On the western side were the Teton Sioux with seven subnations. They lived in tipis which they disassembled for travel and carried behind horses or dogs in supports called travois. They were nomadic and followed the buffalo. The explorers met three Teton Sioux chiefs: Partisan, Buffalo Medicine, and Black Buffalo. Black Buffalo came to the rescue of the expedition when the other Indians tried to steal a pirogue, a long narrow canoe, and all its cargo. His warriors slept on the shore and in boats as Black Buffalo had ordered.

## ESSENTIAL INDIAN HELP

Contrary to the notion that the explorers would meet cruel, sub-human savages, they had met many friendly tribes who fed, advised, and guided them. Indeed, without the help of Indians, the expedition party might not have survived. More than forty tribes were studied. Documented for the first time were the cultures of the Shoshone, Flathead, Nez Perce, and Walla Walla. Contact with other important tribes were the Oto, Missouri, Yankton Sioux, Teton Sioux, Cheyenne, Arikara, Mandan, Crow, Hidatsa, Blackfeet, Wanapam, Chinook and Clatsop.

*Lewis and Clark continued on page 8*

*continued from page 7*

# LEWIS & CLARK

## THE FIRST WINTER

The winter of 1804-05 was spent at Fort Mandan among the Hidatsa and Mandan villages (about 4,000 people). A French trapper, Charbonneux, and his young wife Sacagawea joined the expedition at this time. She gave birth to Jean Pierre, a beloved youngster nicknamed "Pomp" by Clark. Their keel boat left for St. Louis in April, loaded with scientific samples and data. The corps had made six new canoes during the winter. They headed west and spotted the Rocky Mountains on May 26, 1805. They met the Shoshones as they entered the mountains and traded for badly needed horses. From the Lolo Trail in Montana they crossed the Bitterroot Mountains. This was one of the hardest parts of the adventure. Game was scarce and temperatures were frigid.

## THE PACIFIC OCEAN

The Nez Perce generously fed the starving men and guided them to the Columbia River. On November 18, 1805 they reached the Pacific Ocean. Clark said,"We arrived in Sight of the Great Western (for I cannot say Pacific) Ocean as I have not seen one pacific day since my arrival in its vicinity." Fort Clatsop was built on a bluff. They lived here for 4½ months with only 12 rain-free days.

Time at Fort Clatsop was miserable. Fleas tormented them, fevers and colds were common, their food was spoiled. Salt helped make their food taste better so a group spent days boiling sea water until the pots were coated with sea salt. They managed to try to harvest a beached whale but the Indians had completed the task so they bought what the Indians would sell. They spent hundreds of hours sewing new clothes of skins that replaced their worn out ones. They made 338 pairs of moccasins. Clark worked on maps and Lewis described hundreds of plants and animals new to science. He also wrote accounts about Indian customs, dress and life-styles.

## YORK, CLARK'S SERVANT

One notable member of the Corps was York, Clark's African-American slave. He had been Clark's servant since boyhood and probably had a wife and family before leaving for the expedition. Many Indian warriors painted themselves with black soot to indicate exceptional bravery and the taking of scalps, but they were fascinated with York's skin color that did not wash off. York had full equality with other members: he voted, hunted, carried weapons, and was one of the most skilled hunters. However, after the expedition, every member received money and land for their services. York received nothing. After his experience on the adventure, resuming slavery was unbearable to him, yet Clark refused to give him his freedom.

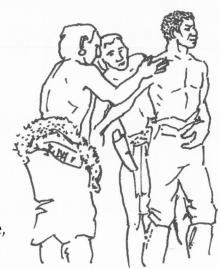

## SEAMAN, LEWIS' DOG

Lewis' dog, Seaman, was the 120 pound Newfoundland dog who was both amusing and helpful as an expert hunter and watchdog. He could sniff out a bear or a buffalo before any human was aware it was nearby. To the Indians he was a curiosity as he more closely resembled a bear than a dog.

## JOURNEY'S END

On March, 1806, the expedition left its winter quarters and headed back toward the United States. The Walla Walla chief Yelleppit replenished their supplies while Clark paid for the goods in medical services. They then spent a month with the Nez Perce at Camp Chopunnish from May 14 to June 10th. Once again Clark set up a thriving medical practice treating up to 50 Indians a day. When they started to cross the Rocky Mountains the snow was fifteen feet deep! They tried again on June 24 with Indian guides and reached Travelers' Rest (in today's Montana) in six days.

The Corps of Discovery arrived in St. Louis in September of 1806, only to find that they had been given up for lost. They had survived an 8,000 mile journey losing only one member to illness, not violence. They had been gone 2 years, 4 months, and 10 days. They had collected and recorded information on 58 different American Indian tribes, 122 animals and 178 plants. They had successfully completed one of the most difficult experiences of exploration ever attempted.

Sacagawea

# Sacagawea

## SACAGAWEA (SAH-CAH-GAH-WE-A) AND HER JOURNEY WITH LEWIS AND CLARK

*Materials: A 10" paper plate (Chinette™ brand works well), 7" x 16" white poster board or file folder, 2" x 9½" poster board stand, 1" x 6" movable arm (if a folder is used, 2" x 6" arm doubled for strength), scissors, stapler, 2 paper fasteners. Pattern on page 72.*

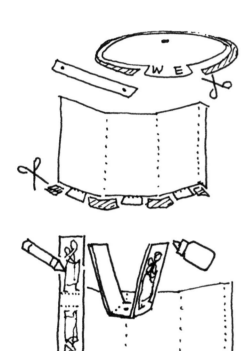

1. Trim edge from plate leaving a 2" tab as a handle and a stop for the figure. Mark E for east on right side of tab and W for west on left side. Poke hole in center of plate. Punch holes in each end of 6" arm about ¼" from ends. Fold 16" Corps of Discovery panel into three 5" sections with a 1" edge. Cut off bottom inch except for a 2" tab on each section to be stapled to the plate.

2. Color and glue Sacagawea and Pomp (her infant son) to 2" x 9½" stand. Fold on dotted lines. Poke hole in center of ½" open space. On the three sections draw and color some amazing things she would have seen on her Corps of Discovery adventure.

3. Turn plate over. Lay 6" arm under plate matching center hole with hole in plate top. Fasten with paper fastener. Fold 1" edge under first section of Corps panel and staple from top and bottom. Staple each of three panel tabs to plate. Finish by adding color to plate.

4. Push paper fastener through holes to attach Sacagawea stand to arm. Press together at top and tape. Guide Sacagawea and Pomp from east to west through their grand wilderness adventure. Stopping at the western tab turn them about-face and return to the east.

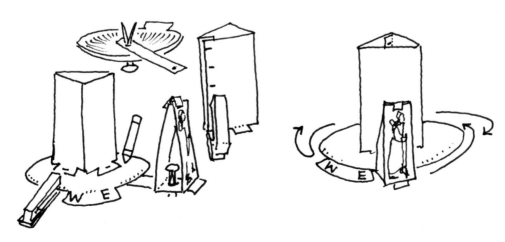

*Sacagawea continued on page 68*

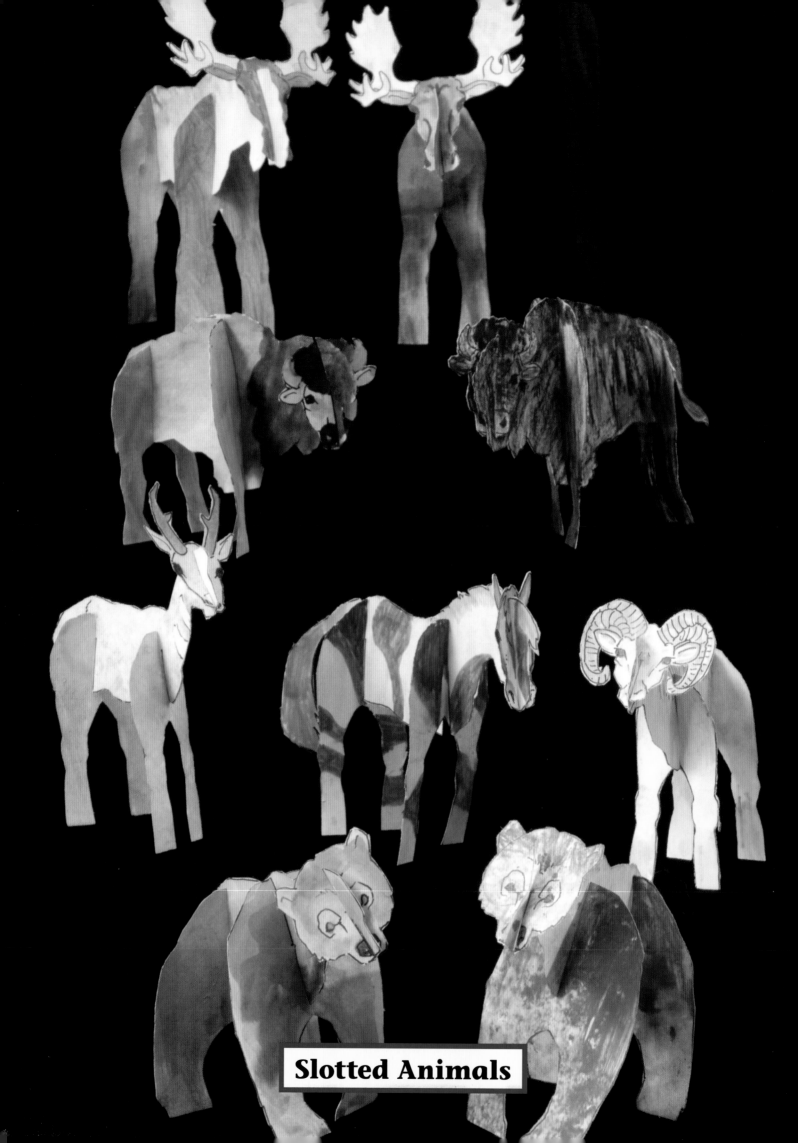

**Slotted Animals**

ART • SCIENCE • SCULPTURE

# Slotted Animals

*Materials: Any type of cardboard that can be easily cut but will hold attached pieces such as poster board or manila folders. Any art supplies such as paint, markers, oil pastels, crayons, and scissors. Patterns on pages 74–75.*

1. Find the patterns for slotted animals. Enlarge them on a copy machine.

2. Cut out the animal with all of its parts and trace around them onto a piece of cardboard. Darken features on the pattern by rubbing the paper with the side of a graphite pencil and then tracing the lines, transferring them to the cardboard.

4. Study pictures of the animal. Notice the different colors on the underbelly, ears, nose, and tail. Color the surface of the animal, back and front of each part.

5. Slot the animals together. You can reduce the pattern pieces to make animal babies.

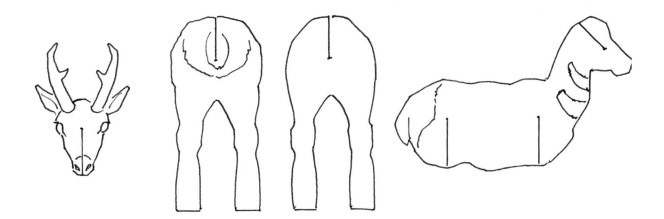

## ADD TEXTURE TO THE ANIMAL SURFACES WITH THESE TECHNIQUES:

Cover paper with thick crayon and then scratch it with a nail.
A third step might be to paint over the scratched area.

1. Lightly daub with a paint-filled brush/toothbrush which is called "stippling" and looks like fur.

2. Make paint dots by dipping eraser point into paint.

3. Make dots or patterns with glue, let it dry, and paint over it.

4. Dip a corner of a small sponge into paint and lightly daub.

**Salmon Ball & Cup Game**

# Salmon Ball & Cup Game

## EASY HUMPBACK SALMON GAME

*Materials: One toilet paper tube, plain white paper 10" x 4", red, orange-brown, brown, black, turquoise crayons or oil pastels, scissors, black fine and heavy tipped markers, pencil, eraser, two feet of string, glue, a heavy bead or button, black paint and big bristle brush. Patterns on page 73.*

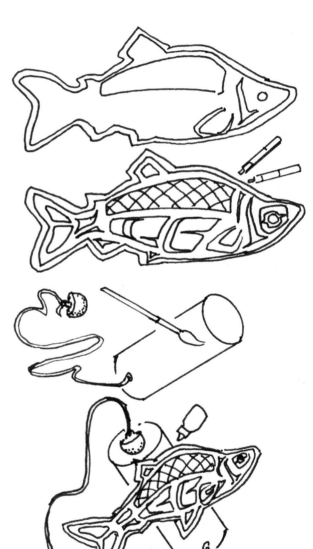

1. Draw the salmon on the paper paying close attention to the colors and designs. Be original with your salmon but know that the Northwest Coast Indians followed a strict formula for designs and color.

2. Outline the designs in thin black marker. Outline the body in a heavy black marker. Color the salmon. Every space should be colored. Cut the salmon out.

3. Punch a hole at the bottom of the tube with a scissors tip. Paint the outside of the tube black. Let it dry. Push the string through the tube hole and knot it. Knot a bead/button on the other end. Glue the salmon onto the middle of the tube.

## MORE DIFFICULT DOG SALMON GAME

Follow the materials list and instructions 1–3. The difference between the two projects is that the dog salmon is a more complex design (thus more authentic), drawn on poster board with markers, and the string is three feet long, making the game more challenging.

When Lewis and Clark reached the Columbia River they met the "salmon-culture" Indians: the Chinook and Clatsop. These natives shared the design forms of northern tribes such as the Kwakiutl and Haida.

This is not a true Northwest Coast Indian Game. However, most Native American cultures played a "ring and pin" game as did most cultures in the world. In Mexico it is called Balero and in English, Bilbocatch.

**Two Dwellings**

# Two Dwellings

## THE EARTH LODGE

*Materials: An oatmeal box or 2½" cylinder, 6"–7" paper bowl, 4 Popsicle™ sticks cut in half, 1½" x 6½" poster board or folder strip, paintbrush, thinned white glue, 1–3" strips of paper towel, brown paint, scissors, tape. Pattern on page 72.*

1. Trim edges of paper bowl to 5¼"–5½" diameter leaving three tabs to attach to cylinder. Cut chimney hole in center of bowl. Tape bowl to cylinder.

2. For lodge entry make two vertical cuts 2" high and 1½" apart in cylinder. Bend up door. On folder strip mark ½", 2", 1½", 2", ½". Fold on marks and glue ½" edges to underside of cardboard for supported doorway.

3. Tear paper towels into 1"–3" strips. Brush lodge with glue a section at a time and layer paper all over the lodge top and entry...except for sides of entry which must remain smooth. Allow to dry.

4. Paint lodge brown. Leave sides of entrance unpainted. Dry. Glue four Popsicle™ stick "logs" to sides of entry.

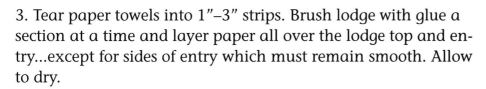

## THE TIPI

*Materials: A piece of corrugated cardboard 8" x 10", a piece of freezer paper 8" x 10" discolored with strong tea, six 11½" skewer sticks with points snipped off, a twist tie, 3 toothpicks, a 7" circle form, scissor point or hole punch for making holes for tipi sticks.*

*Two Dwellings continued on page 70*

**Northwest Coast Canoe**

# Northwest Coast Canoe

*Materials: White poster board 24" x 15", enlarged pattern, orange-brown paint wash for canoe outside and inside, two black markers, medium point and wide point, orange-red markers (same points), scissors, glue, masking tape, brush, pencil and eraser, stylized patterns from this Indian culture. Pattern on page 73.*

1. Enlarge canoe pattern the desired size. Lay the three patterns on the poster board: front of the boat, back, and bottom. Cut out the three pieces and see that they line up. Pinch both ends together and push out the middle to see that the bottom will fit.

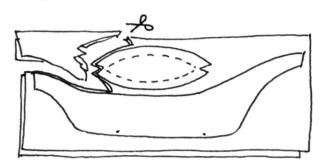

2. Draw the stylized designs with a pencil, studying examples of Northwest Coast art. Our sample canoe has a raven motif. When you have filled the poster board front with a design, apply the black and orange-red marker with thick, medium, and thin lines. All space was filled with a form, often repeated and varied.

3. Prepare the orange-brown paint (meant to resemble cedarwood) with a very diluted wash and brush it over all poster board pieces, back and front.

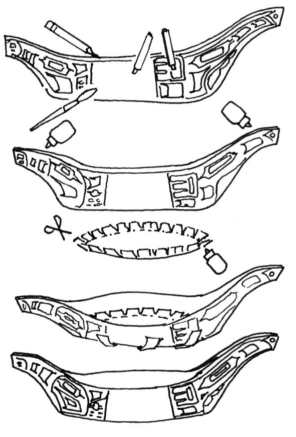

4. After the paint wash has dried, glue both ends of the boat together leaving a third on each end to give the boat double strength. Notch ¼" around the oval boat bottom. Fold each notch up. Test the notched bottom piece by slipping it from the open top to the bottom. It does not have to be a perfect fit, but enough for the boat to be supported.

5. Remove the notched piece. Lay it out on a protected surface. Glue the notches so they will attach to the inside surface of the boat. Once the piece is in place, put strips of masking tape on the outside to temporarily hold the awkward bottom in place. Let the glue dry overnight. Gently pull the masking tape from the boat. Some touch-up work may have to be done. Stand your handsome boat up. These canoes were truly works of art.

**On October 23, 1805, Lewis and Clark visited their first Chinook village and saw their first Chinookan canoe made of pine, remarkably light, wide in the middle, and tapering to each end with crosspieces that made the craft surprisingly strong.**

# PIONEERS

## WESTWARD MOVEMENT

With the now-famous phrase "Go west, young man!" the westward movement commenced in the early 1840s. A steady stream of men, women, and children packed their essential belongings and left Independence, Missouri in covered wagons. From a distance the long wagon line resembled a flotilla of boats, and the wagons were soon named "prairie schooners." The four- to six-month journey cost a family from $700 to $1,500 dollars with most members walking part of the 2,000-mile trek. The travelers were trappers, missionaries, European emigrants, and Americans searching for religious freedom or the fertile paradise promised by promoters, word-of-mouth, and the government.

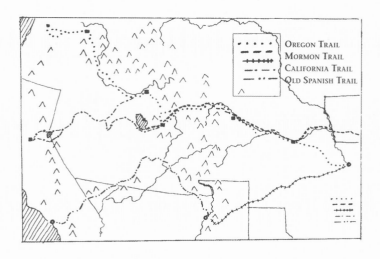

OREGON TRAIL
MORMON TRAIL
CALIFORNIA TRAIL
OLD SPANISH TRAIL

## THE TRAILS

Settlers followed many different trails on their westward move. Beginning in Independence, Missouri and ending at Fort Vancouver, Washington, the Oregon Trail was the main westward route. This trail paralleled much of the Mormon Trail which also began at Independence but ended at the Great Salt Lake Valley. A third route, the California Trail, turned south to Sacramento. From there, the Old Spanish Trail extended to Los Angeles. Yet another famous route, the Santa Fe Trail, started in Independence and ended in Santa Fe, New Mexico. Though the traveler had several trail options, no route avoided the forbidding mountains, pitiless deserts, and Indians. The Great Basin of Utah and Nevada was an especially treacherous part of the trail. Here settlers faced 200,000 square miles of white, salty sand, baked clay and the intense reflection off the Great Salt Lake. A California-bound woman wrote, "I have suffered more this afternoon than all my sufferings put together." Once through the Rocky Mountains and South Pass, Wyoming, the Oregon settlers separated from the Utah and California bound groups.

## THE OXEN

Oxen were used to move settlers westward. Less expensive and easier to train than horses, oxen also adjusted more easily to extreme temperatures, were less likely to be stolen, and were less susceptible to disease. An oxen, with hooves shod for better traction, could steadily pull a heavy load over rough ground during the journey as well as till the ground and haul lumber, stone, and rock once the destination was reached. Linked in two to three teams per wagon, they covered an average of twelve miles a day.

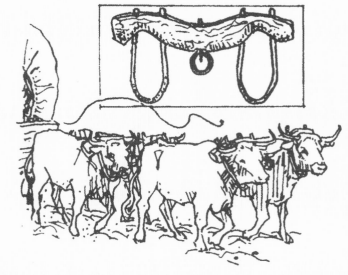

## LOADING THE COVERED WAGON

Covered wagons moved 1,000 pounds of food, cooking utensils, bedding, clothing, weapons, and tools over the western terrain. The wheels were removable and the canvas was waterproofed with linseed oil for river crossings. Selecting, weighing, and loading provisions impacted a family's ability to survive during the crossing. Only a few cherished family albums, china pieces, or furniture items could accompany the family to their new home.

Trouble with Indians was rare and trading usually consisted of a peaceable exchange of clothing, ironware, and furnishings in exchange for buffalo meat and food staples. Accidents and disease were more common traveling hazards. One out of 17 travelers, or 6% died on the trail. Cholera was the most common cause of death. Accidental gunshot wounds also took their toll.

CROSSING RIVERS     BUFFALO STAMPEDES     CLIMBING MOUNTAINS     REPAIRING WAGONS

## THE PIONEER HOME

Even after the settlers reached their final destination, the covered wagon continued to provide shelter. Temporary tents helped with overflow, but often months passed before a crude dugout home was ready for winter occupancy. If timber was scarce, clay bricks or sod cuttings were used to fashion makeshift homes. Often, several years would pass before timber cabins were built. However by the turn of the century, fine Victorian homes and mansions dotted the frontier.

TENT

SOD HOME

## DAILY LIFE ON THE FRONTIER

The settlers learned to improvise. Soap was made from lye and fat; dye was made from bark and plants; tea was brewed from sage and salves from yarrow root. Carrots and boiled sugar were combined to make jam. Eyewash was made from gunpowder dissolved in water; onions mashed in sugar became cough syrup; and goose grease and turpentine were used as a poultice for the chest during a cold. A Spokane, Washington settler wrote to his friends in Maine detailing daily chores: "digging wells, herding livestock, gardening, making shoes, butchering meat, dipping candles, making soap, baking bread, washing clothes, sewing, milking cows, and raising children."

LOG HOME

STANDARD HOME

A pioneer wrote about early times in Oregon country: "I never saw so fine a population as in Oregon. They were honest, because there was nothing to steal; sober, because there was no liquor; there were no misers because there was no money; and industrious because it was work or starve." The settlers were naive about the trials presented by "going west." Nonetheless, they faced each obstacle with determined heroism and ultimately succeeded in the new frontier.

**A Simple Sunbonnet**

# A Simple Sunbonnet

*Materials: Paper plate, rectangular piece of cloth or crepe paper (it must be large enough to cover the wearer's head), stapler, glue, ribbons for ties, scissors, markers or crayons, additional ribbon for streamers are optional.*

1. Put the paper plate faceup. To make the rim of the bonnet, cut a wedge from the paper plate and cut out the center of the plate as shown. Decorate the front part of the rim.

2. Make small triangle-shaped cuts along the inside edge of the rim; bend the tabs back.

3. To make the back drape of the bonnet, gather the long side of the rectangular cloth or paper and staple it to the tabs. If you are using paper, you might glue it to the tabs.

4. On the sides of the bonnet, bring the cloth edges A and B together to make a tuck. Staple the tuck to ends of the rim to create a head shape for the sunbonnet. Staple the ribbons as ties.

Head coverings were not only decorative but necessary for the pioneers. Sunbonnets shielded the women's eyes from the sun, wind, and dust. The back drape protected the neck. They were made from inexpensive calico or denim.

Men wore hats made from skins or hides. Both men and women made straw hats from locally grown straw that was braided and then sewn into a hat.

**Hop-Along Hobbyhorse**

# Hop-Along Hobbyhorse

*Materials: A large, clean, knee-high sock of any natural color, a 1"thick dowel about 36" long, yarn for the mane, 4 buttons or 4 brown felt circles (2 for eyes and 2 for nostrils), felt for ears, embroidery floss for facial details such as mouth and eyelashes, glue, batting for the sock head, needle with a large eye, rawhide laces or string for reins, thread (optional, used for sewing on buttons for eyes and nostrils).*

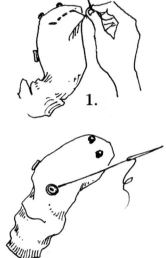

1. Attach felt eyes and nose by putting your hand inside the sock. Glue or sew eyes and nostrils in place. Make the mouth with a running in-and-out stitch along the sock toe seam.

2. Cut the felt ears. Make a pleat in the ears by folding felt from point A to point B. Sew ears on each side of the head.

3. To make the mane, thread yarn into a large-eyed needle. Loop at the base of each strand. Cut loops. Stuff sock head with batting or old nylons. You will have to stuff tightly to avoid a limp and floppy horse.

**1.**

4. Place the dowel end into the batting at least 8"–10" inches. To keep batting enclosed, glue legend of sock to dowel. Grasp the glued section firmly while it dries or wrap it with several rubber bands. Let glue dry overnight. Add reins of string or rawhide shoelaces. Wrap reins several times around the sock base.

**2.**

fold

A B

**3.**

**4.**

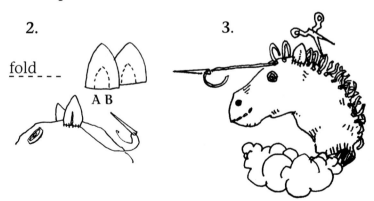

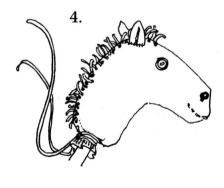

Horses were not just a luxury to early settlers, they were also a necessity for work and transportation. Western horses had strong lungs from breathing mountain air. The dry climate contributed to stronger hooves and their muscles were powerful from long travels. Imaginative children fashioned horses from everyday materials, often making heads and bodies from socks, carved wood, or bunched twigs.

Punch-A-Can Lantern

# Punch-A-Can Lantern

*Materials: Any size empty, lidless, tin can (a 16 oz. or 29 oz. size works well), water, freezer, nail hammer, pencil, paper, masking tape, old towel, black spray paint, a short candle, wire for handle (optional).*

1. Wash the can and fill it with water. Freeze until the water is solid ice. Remove the can from the freezer. Draw your idea for a design on paper you have cut to fit the can and wrap it around the can.

2. Lay the can on a folded cloth towel and punch out the design. Remove paper and tape. Let ice melt enough so that it can be removed from the can.

3. Place your lantern upside down on a protected surface and spray it with black spray paint. Let the paint dry. Work in a well-ventilated area only!

4. Place the candle in the lantern. You may wish to make a wire handle. Light candle and admire your glowing design in a darkened space.

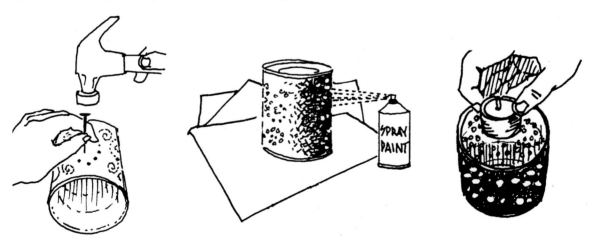

This tin can is useful and fun. Pioneers punched tin lanterns to give more light and add decoration to their homes. Punched tinware such as cupboards, boxes, and chests were popular storage items and are now favored antiques from this historical period.

**Pounded Plant Prints**

# Pounded Plant Prints

*Materials: Several pages of plain ink-free newsprint or other thin paper for practicing before you go to fabric; fresh-picked leaves of as many different plants as possible, hammer or fist-sized flat rock, 100% cotton fabric, washing soda (can be purchased from the supermarket), a hard surface for hammering such as cement or a strong wooden surface.*

1. Gather the plants. Choose thin, flat leaves. Chose bright-colored flowers such as pansies, rose petals, forget-me-nots, violas. Remember you never know how the flower dye is going to transfer to the paper or fabric. The surprise is part of the fun. Ivy, shamrock, geranium, and rose leaves work quite well. Purple and red-colored flowers make a nice contrast but sometimes turn blue in the soda.

2. Cover a hard surface with newsprint pages to test the plants on. Test on fabric scraps as well. Place a leaf or flower facedown on the fabric. Cover the fabric with one or two layers of paper. Hammer the newsprint touching the entire surface. Carefully lift the protective paper and see if the tannin of the leaf or flower transferred to the surface.

3. Dip the finished cloth into a solution of soda and water (½ cup soda to 2 cups water). The tannin of the plants "fixes" with the solution (it may also change color). After "fixing" the colors wash the fabric gently in soapy water, rinse, and dry.

You might try to make a leaf and flower "sampler" as pioneer girls made samplers by stitching the alphabet. The finished sampler was usually prominently displayed in the home. One pioneer girl wrote of her sampler days, "Aunt Nancy reeled the silk from some cocoons and dyed skeins which we used for our embroidery. When finished we framed them. For years the Lord's Prayer, The Ten Commandments and God Bless Our Home were ever before us."

Practical as well as decorative, samplers taught children sewing skills which were applied to lace-making, mending, darning, hemming, and tatting (a type of lacework). Usually a sampler was begun to practice the ABCs. Sometimes a family tree was sewn by weaving family hair into the stitches.

# Three Settler Dolls

## CORN HUSK DOLL

*Materials: Pioneers used fresh, washed corn husks and corn silk for the hair. We have found tamale wrappers work well. Scissors, string or yarn, scraps of cloth, glue, bits of printed fabric, a smal tissue ball.*

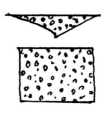

1. Choose three wrappers, laying them one over another. Roll a small tissue ball and place it in the center of the husks. Fold the corn husks evenly around the ball to make a head. Tie firmly at the neck.

2. Make arms from a narrow piece of tightly rolled husk. Fold two ends so they overlap in the middle. This middle part will be held in place by the doll's body.

3. Wrap waist of doll with string. Dress the doll with a bright kerchief and apron. Glue it in place. Add yarn or corn silk hair.

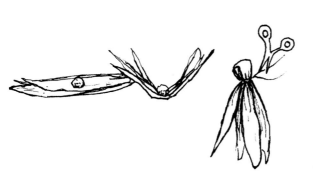

## TWIG DOLL

*Materials: A twig with branches forked like arms and legs or two twigs tied together, a nut (we used a walnut, acorn, or hazelnut) for the head, scraps of cloth, a hot-glue gun or good craft glue, paint of permanent markers for the face, yarn for hair, an electric drill with a small bit for drilling into the nut and mounting the nut on the stick top (essential if you are working with a group).*

1. Find your twig. Use good scissors or pruning shears to make a clean cut. Cut out printed cloth for clothes using these simple patterns. If your stick lacks arms or legs, attach them with yarn as shown. Cut a neck opening in shirt fabric. Slip shirt over "neck."

2. Attach head with a hot glue gun. Use the drill if you have one. Paint or draw the face. Gather the shirt at the waist and tie it in place. Glue skirt over shirt. Glue on the scarf.

## HANKIE DOLL

*Materials: An iron, square pieces of muslin or cotton cloth (any size square; our doll is made from a 10" x 10" square), thread, needle, straight pins, scissors, cotton ball the size of an apricot, cotton swab, small calico print or any printed fabric scraps.*

1. Wash and iron your piece of cloth. Lay out cloth. Fold up a ½" hem and iron it. Gather each corner and wrap thread around the gathers. You are making hands and feet that are each about ½" long.

2. Place a cotton ball in the center of the square and gather in the neck. Wrap thread around the neck and tie firmly. Cut the ends.

3. Push and pull the fabric until you can see two arms in front and two legs behind. Pin, hem, and sew the back using a slip stitch.

4. For a kerchief cut a triangle 4"–5" wide at the longest side. For an apron, cut a 3"–5" square. With a needle and thread gather the apron at the top and sew ends together at back. Give the doll cross-stitched eyes and pink cheeks (with makeup blush on a cotton swab.

It is astonishing to learn of the crude materials pioneers lovingly cut and combined to create a doll. One story tells of a rag doll made from clothing found in a shallow grave. But the doll had to be taken away and the child placed under quarantine. The clothing had belonged to cholera victims traveling on the western trail.

Tops

# Tops

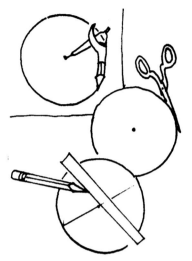

*Materials: Poster board or a file folder, 2"–3" round lid, ruler, scissors, pencil, colored markers, masking tape, nail or heavy toothpick with pointed ends for spinning.*

1. On the cardboard draw several circles with a compass, or trace around a lid. Make small circles. Tops over 3" in diameter don't spin well. Mark the center using a ruler.

2. Cut out your tops. With a pencil and a ruler divide each top into sections: halves, thirds, quarters, and so on.

3. Use markers to draw designs similar to the pioneer designs shown or use your own ideas. You may repeat the same design several times or alternate designs in the sectioned parts.

4. Press the nail or toothpick through the center hole. Spin. If the spinner begins to slip, attach pieces of masking tape to keep it in place.

## AN EASY SCIENCE PROJECT

Try a science project in mixing colors. If you color one top half red and half blue, what color will you see when you spin the top? The colors have to be quite strong for this to work. Try it. If you guessed purple, you are correct. Remember that yellow and blue make the secondary color green, and red and yellow make orange.

During the long journey across the plains, pioneer children cherished their pocket toys. One boy carried a small wooden top. The boy's wagon train cared for a lost Indian child. The lonesome boy was fascinated with the top and a friendship developed between the two. Weeks later, when the Indian child's family was found, the pioneer boy gave the Indian child his treasured top.

**Veggie Prints**

# Veggie Prints

*Materials: Hard vegetables (such as potatoes, carrots, turnips, sweet potatoes), a small safe knife or sharp pencil, acrylic or tempera paint, sponge, rag or inexpensive brush, water, cloth or paper, tray for paint.*

1. Choose your vegetable. Potatoes work best. Slice the vegetable lengthwise.

2. Draw a design by digging into the veggie surface with a sharp pencil. With the knife carve away the sides so that the design is about ¼" higher than the edge. Some design ideas might be a sun, a flower or leaf, a butterfly, your first name initial, etc.

3. Pour the paint into an inexpensive foil pan or paper plate. If your paint container is lined with foil, cleanup is quick and easy. You may want to smooth out the paint using a roller. This is optional.

4. Press the image into the paint or brush the paint onto the image with a sponge, rag, or brush. Stamp the image on the paper you are decorating. Test your stamp on scrap paper before you print on the final paper surface.

5. Let the stamped image dry.

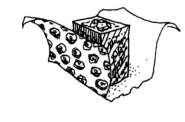

6. Use the printed design paper to wrap gifts or display in your home or classroom.

Roll the paint.

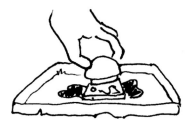
press carved surface onto the paint

or brush the paint on.

**Vegetables can be cut, carved, brushed with paint, and then stamped on paper or cloth for a variety of uses. Vegetables are inexpensive, accessible, safe to carve, and easy for small hands to hold.**

*Veggie Prints continued on page 69*

**Rubbings**

# Rubbings

*Materials: Dark-colored crayons with the paper removed, lightweight white or cream-colored paper, tape, surfaces with raised patterns and pictures.*

1. Rubbings are traditionally made in graveyards* where a tombstone often has a stone-carved image such as a weeping willow or flowers. You can discover interesting information about early settlers in your area by visiting a cemetery with your rubbing equipment. Watch for horizontal or vertical surfaces from which you can take a rubbing. *Permission must be granted from the cemetery sexton to do this project.*

2. Peel off the paper from the crayons. Break them in half.

3. Tape the paper to the surface of the rubbing image. Rub the side of the crayon over the paper. Perhaps the narrow tip of the crayon will work better.

4. What fun to watch the carved image show up on the paper.

Try rubbing coins, fossils, patterned dishes, silverware, manhole covers, shells, medals, keys, and textured surfaces you have discovered.

Rag Rug

# Rag Rug

*Materials: A piece of stiff cardboard for a loom (6" x 6" is a good beginning size), 11½ yards of strong cotton thread, patterned cotton scraps, scissors for cutting cloth, a ruler, pencil, and a fork to "beat down" the rug weft.*

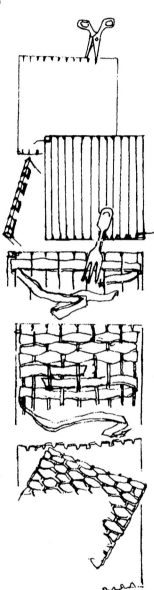

1. Prepare rags by cutting 1" strips. Consider complementary colors: red and green, blue and orange, yellow and purple.

2. Make a "loom" with your piece of cardboard. Mark for slots 1/2" apart on edges of board. Cut slots 1/8" deep.

3. Warp the loom by securely tying warp string around the first slot. Continue wrapping warp string up and down and around top and bottom slots. Finish by tying warp tightly around last slot.

4. Begin weaving the rug. Start with a rag strip as long as your arm. Weave end backwards over and under across the loom. Fold. Tuck edges under so the woven strip has a neat appearance. Beat down woven strip with a fork.

5. Continue weaving until you run out of the color or wish to change color. To add a new strip overlap 3 or 4 warp threads with the new rag strip. Continue weaving and beating. Your rug is finished when no more folded strips can be woven in. Tuck the last end underneath and tie off.

6. Fold down the slotted edges and slide the rug off the loom. Adjust weft so it is even.

Rag rugs, woven on large looms, were colorful, practical floor coverings. Women often gathered with friends to prepare rag rugs much as they did for quilt making. After cutting the strips and sewing the ends, the rags would be rolled into a ball. The patterned fabric weft, woven into bright and sturdy warps, made a durable welcoming carpet.

Cattle Brand Quilt

# Cattle Brand Quilt

*Materials: Cloth or paper with a small pattern such as origami, gift wrap, or wallpaper sample books, pencil, ruler, scissors, black tempera or acrylic paint, glue, fabric paint in tube.*

1. Choose a simple quilt pattern such as a log cabin design. Enlarge the square to the desired size. The square must have some empty space for the brand.

2. Cut a template for each different shape in your pattern. Carefully trace as many of each as you need. Cut out shapes. Exact measuring and cutting is necessary in order for shapes to fit together.

3. Assemble the quilt pieces on light or white backing paper. Glue in place.

4. Decide on the brands. The pictured quilt has a "Flying A" and a "Bar H".

5. Test the brands on scrap paper or fabric using the tube paint. Lightly draw the brand on the quilt section. Paint it in black with a brush and paint or tube application.

A brand was a symbol of ownership that was burned on all livestock with a hot metal tool called a branding iron. As personal as a coat of arms, the brand legally belonged to a specific ranch. Brands were painted on ranch buildings, tooled in leather, and stamped into silver.

Quilts are a unique American art form. To escape the loneliness of frontier life, women often gathered to form quilting bees. Quilts were then passed on from generation to generation. In 1995, Edith Gentry of Roosevelt, Utah introduced a novel addition to quilt making. She used livestock brands that had been important to her as artistic symbols. With her permission we have adapted her idea to this quilt project.

# PLAINS INDIANS

## THE LAND

The Plains Indian country is grasslands, valleys and hills. Summers were hot and winters severely cold. The wild game furnished Indians with food. Buffalo was a main food and cultural resource. The religion and art were shaped by their surroundings.

Recent archeological studies indicate that man has lived on the Plains for more than 10,000 years. Called Paleo-Indians, these early people hunted buffalo and mammoths using spears with chipped flint arrowheads. About 6,000 years ago the climate changed to a hotter, drier one and animals and people moved north and west.

Today the Great Plains, the heartland of North America, is 2,500 miles long and 600 miles wide. The western boundary is formed by the Rocky Mountains and to the north, flatlands extend to Alberta and Manitoba in Canada. The eastern boundary is the Missouri/Mississippi rivers and the prairie terrain. The southern line follows the Rio Grande but not so far as the Gulf of Mexico.

## HIGH PLAINS TRIBES

The Assiniboin, Ojibwa, Gros Ventre, Crow, Sioux, Arapaho, Cheyenne, Commanche, Kiowa, Apache (Kiowa and Lipan). These tribes were nomadic and lived in tipis which could be dismantled and carried to better hunting land. From 100 to 200 tipis might be tightly grouped as tribes gathered in the spring or summer for ceremonies. In fall and winter the group would break down into smaller sub tribes.

## PRAIRIE TRIBES

The Hidatsa, Mandan, Arikara, Omaha, Ponca, Osage, Pawnee and Wichita. These semi-sedentary people grew crops which they traded for meat. Their tightly grouped clusters of earthen lodges were usually surrounded by a wooden wall and a dry moat.

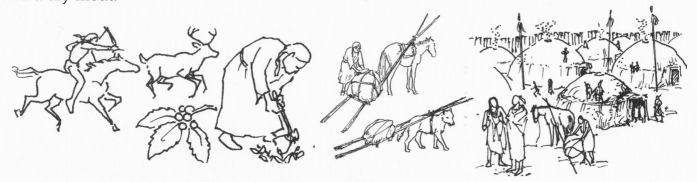

## APPEARANCE AND CULTURE

Plains Indians were a handsome people with bronze skin, strong, white teeth, a prominent, long nose, almost six feet in height, small hands and feet, with their hair generally in braids (men and women). Men had little facial hair. Many Indian men had more than one wife, often depending on their wealth (more horses, more possessions, bigger tipi, more work for one wife, etc.) Children were cherished and desirable. Grandmothers often raised the children as the mothers had demanding duties. Fathers were also important in the child's upbringing. When a boy reached 14 years a right of passage, or "vision quest" was made and a "guardian spirit" sought. Often an animal would appear in the fasting boy's dream. The qualities of that animal transferred to him and had spiritual and artistic meaning in his life.

## RELIGION AND CEREMONIES

Many tribal gatherings combined social and religious celebrations with dancing, storytelling, feasting, gift-giving, courting, speeches and games. These usually took place in the summer when it was easier to travel, there were more trade goods and food, and there was abundant grass for the horses. They believed in many spirits: the Thunderbird ruled the Upper World; the Underwater and Underground were controlled by multiple spirits.

Dancing was important to the ceremonial, spiritual, and social life of the people. It was thought to renew the earth's spirit and the animals and crops as well as maintain the energy and life force of the tribe. Both Warrior Societies and Womens' Guilds hosted their own dances. The following were the most important ceremonies: The *Sun Dance,* which was sacred to all. The *Scalp Dance,* which lasted many days and was held as a celebration of victory over enemies. The *Buffalo Dance* depicted a hunt and was performed by men wearing a buffalo headpiece. It was danced when meat was scarce in order to bring the herds closer to the village. During the dance young men left the village to scout for buffalo.

## FOOD

Indians had to hunt, grow and collect all their food. They had to figure out how to preserve and store food during winter and hard times. Essential foods included the prairie turnip which was dug out of the ground. It is thought that there were 60,000,000 buffalo 200 years ago. Five hundred different plants were eaten and used for flavoring, healing, and teas. Meat was dried on rocks in the sun or hung from wooden scaffolding. So were fish and other game. Pemmican, a nutritious portable protein-rich food, was made from powdered, dried meat and dried berries.

continued from page 43

# PLAINS INDIANS

## WOMEN AND CHILDREN

The major role of Plains women was maintaining the household and bearing the children. In the farming societies they also tended the fields, planting and harvesting the crops. In nomadic/hunter tribes they helped butcher the animal, brought the meat into camp, prepared the hides and meat for future use. Women had considerable status as they controlled these services. They were deeply involved in some ceremonies, had expressed opinions about war and sometimes sat on councils. Women also built the tipis and dissassembled them for moving camp.

It was usual for the bride's family to provide a tipi and most of the furnishings such as backrests and beds, cooking and eating utensils. An 1850 trader wrote,"Women were the greatest wealth an Indian possessed next to his horse." Children played hard: in dry weather they played on the hard-packed earth between lodges; in the winter sledding was fun using a simple sled made of rawhide curved at the front. Buffalo ribs roped together made sturdy sleds. In the spring, boys played the hoop game. One team threw hoops laced with rawhide into the air and the other team attempted to catch them on poles.

## THE WAY OF THE WARRIOR

In the late 1700s a fur trader reported, "This is a delightful country, and were it not for perpetual wars, the natives might be the happiest people on earth." When one successful war-party returned, another set off. Horses were the main plunder, stolen from enemies along the way. Warriors took great delight in relating their adventures in war. The status of a Plains Indian family pivoted firmly on achievements of the man. Prestige was gained socially in religion, in acts of generosity such as giving to the poor or giving horses and other goods to visitors in a "give-away", and in tribally approved war. Individuals not interested in the war-path could gain standing by owning certain medicine bundles or taking on the role of a Holy Man.

Before the war party left camp they separated and painted their faces and bodies, horses and regalia. Then they entered their camp singing rehearsed songs and doing victory dances. If scalps had been taken, some of the returning warriors rode into camp with their faces painted black, thus symbolizing that they had taken a scalp.

# TIME LINE OF 100 YEARS

| | |
|---|---|
| 1779–1881 | Smallpox epidemic. |
| 1800–1830 | Fur-trade era begins. Many areas overhunted and trapped by Indian and white trappers alike. |
| 1804–1806 | The Lewis and Clark Voyage of Discovery explores the Upper Missouri and the Rocky Mountains and lands leading to the Pacific Ocean. |
| 1805–1807 | Zebulon Pike searches for the source of the Missisippi and explores the Rocky Mountains. |
| 1811 | John Jacob Astor establishes a fur-trading post in Oregon. |
| 1830 | Congress passes The Indian Removal Act giving President Jackson the power to remove Native Americans from lands in the East to lands west of the Mississippi. |
| 1830–1870 | Buffalo hide trade era: millions of animals killed in order to trade them for guns, metal tools, beads, alcohol and other items. |
| 1833 | Bent's Fort built in southern Colorado for fur trade with the southern and central Plains Indians. |
| 1836–1840 | Smallpox epidemic. |
| 1842–1845 | John Fremont maps the West. |
| 1843 | First wagon train crosses the continent to Oregon. |
| 1845 | John O'Sullivan writes of the United States "Manifest Destiny". |
| 1847 | Marcus and Narcissa Whitman and two other settlers are massacred by Cayuse Indians at their mission in Oregon. The US Army is brought in with the aim of protecting the settlers. The first 247 Mormons enter the valley of the Great Salt Lake. |
| 1848 | Mexico cedes California and the Southwest to the United States. Gold is discovered in California leading to the 1849-50 Gold Rush. |
| 1849 | Fort Laramie, a US Army post, is established at old Fort William in Wyoming. Its purpose is to protect wagon train and Gold Rush immigrants. |
| 1851 | Treaty made at Fort Laramie with Northern Plains Indians. Indians promise not to attack and to receive federal food and supplies. |
| 1853 | Same treaty made with southern Plains Indians at Fort Atkinson. |
| 1854 | Renegade Indians kill 28 people at Grattan. Thereafter, attacks on Overland routes resume. |
| 1856 | Smallpox epidemic. |
| 1857–1870 | Wars between the Plains Indians and US soldiers. Many treaties were signed and reservations of land allotted to various Indian tribes. |
| 1861–1862 | Smallpox epidemic. |
| 1864 | Massacre at Sand Creek. |
| 1866–1868 | Red Cloud leads the Oglala Sioux into war against the US Army over the Bozeman trail area. The government agrees to evacuate forts along the trail. |
| 1869 | The first American Transcontinental Railroad is completed. The power of the Southern Cheyenne Dogmen is broken at the Battle of Summit Springs. |
| 1876 | The Battle of the Little Bighorn, where Sioux and Cheyenne warriors defeat General Custer's troops. State of Colorado joins the Union. |
| 1877 | Chief Joseph of the Nez Perce surrenders to the US Cavalry. Crazy Horse of the Oglala Sioux surrenders and four months later is killed while resisting arrest. |
| 1878–1886 | The last of the great buffalo herds is destroyed and with them the 150-year period of mounted Plains Indian culture. |
| 1881 | Sitting Bull of the Hunkpapa Lakota Sioux surrenders. |
| 1887 | Buffalo Bill's Wild West Show performs for Queen Victoria. |
| 1889 | Two million acres of Indian territory (Oklahoma) are opened to settlers. Montana and North and South Dakota join the Union. |
| 1890 | Battle of Wounded Knee, the end of the American Indian wars. Sitting Bull killed by Indian police. |
| 1896 | State of Utah joins the Union. |
| 1899 | State of Washington joins the Union. |

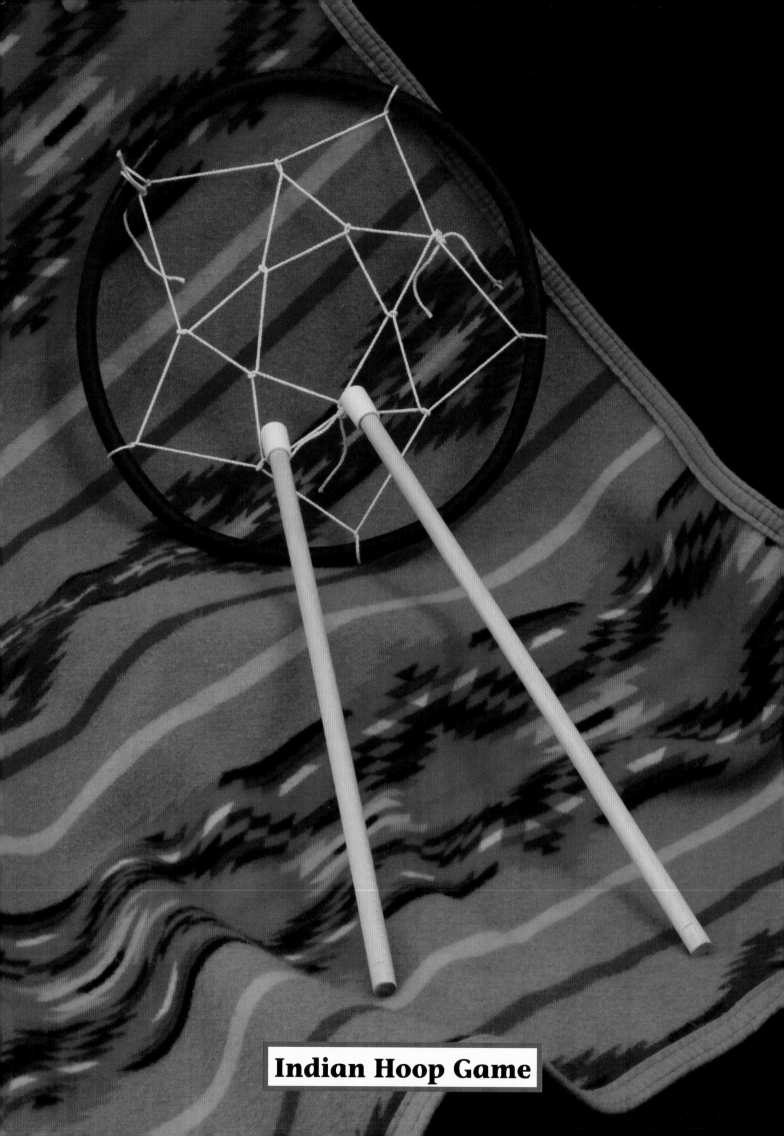

Indian Hoop Game

# Indian Hoop Game

*Materials: For a 12" hoop: 36" flexible tubing (we used ¼" fuel line), black electrical tape, twine, 3"–4" of covered wire almost the size of a hose opening, ½" dowel x 36", cut in half for two darts, two 1/4" leg tips, feathers and yarn, chalk, masking tape.*

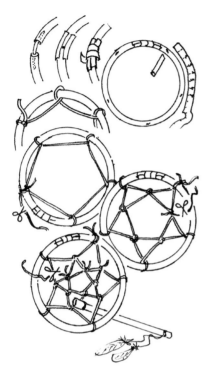

1. Cut two pieces of electrical tape 2" long. Insert connecting wire section into ends of hose and press together. Firmly stick 2" tape strips horizontally above and below the join area. Also tightly wrap center area with more tape to secure the join but not form a bump that will impact a smooth hoop roll.

2. Avoiding the taped join, make five chalk marks around hoop about 7" apart.

3. Our hoop web will be a five-point star. Cut a 40" length of twine. Start first star by choosing a chalk mark and firmly tying twine at the mark. Reach twine to the next mark and wrap around, deliberately coming out underneath the wrap to hold twine in place. The star webbing should be firm but not so tight it distorts the hoop. Continue wrapping and tucking under each wrap. When all five wraps are completed, securely attach twine to first knot and clip off extra.

4. To begin second star cut twine 35". Tie knot to center of one section. Reach to center of next section and wrap around, remembering to come out underneath. Again, your webbing will be firm but not too tight. Continue wrapping center to center until you reach the starting knot. Attach firmly. Clip off extra twine.

5. For the double-star middle, a pentagon, cut twine 30". Tie knot to center of a section, wrap around center of adjoining section and come up underneath. Continue around until you reach the starting knot and tie to it. Clip off extra twine.

6. Prepare throwing darts. Wrap 5" of masking tape around one end of each dowel so tips fit snugly. Add decorative yarn and feathers. Have someone roll hoop. Take turns throwing darts at it aiming for an opening.

**The Plains Indians played games which developed the skills necessary to the successful hunter and warrior. One of these was the hoop game using bent wood and rawhide lacing. Played in various ways by different tribes, the player threw a pole or shot an arrow at a webbed hoop which was rolled along flat ground. Scoring depended on which opening in the web was pierced by the pole. Speed and accuracy determined the winners.**

**Buffalo Headdress & Mask**

# Buffalo Headdress & Mask

## THE HEADDRESS

*Materials: 4" x 9" brown fake, fur (yard of 60" fur can make 15 headpieces); 2½" x 24" poster board or manila file folder for headband; two 4" x 4" squares of poster board for horns; colors: black, brown, grey, ribbons, yarn, crepe paper for streamers, bells, beads, feathers, etc.; glue, paper punch. Pattern on Page 71.*

1. Lay buffalo mane pattern on fur back. Pin and cut. Cut slots for horn. Lay horn pattern on 4" square. Trace around and cut two.

2. Color front of horns black with grey lines. Insert into 3/4" slots. Lay mane with horns face down. Apply glue to back of horn inserts. Position headband over back so bottom edges match and there is a 6" to 7" extension on each side. Lay headband onto back with glued inserts and press firmly on glued areas.

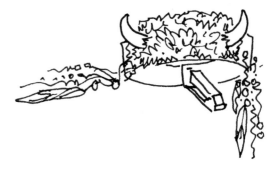

3. Turn headdress over. Punch 2–4 holes on each side behind the ears. Tie in ribbons, feathers, bells etc. Size child's head and staple headband.

## THE BUFFALO MASK

*Materials: A 10" paper plate with outer edge trimmed off (Chinette™ works well). 4½" x 7" brown fake fur, 1½" x 20" poster board/manila folder for headband, 3" x 3" poster board for ears, 2" x 4" poster board for horns; colors: brown, black, grey, scissors, glue, stapler, tape.*

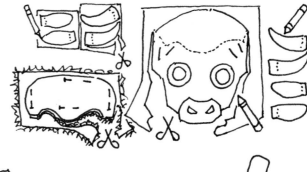

1. Lay horn and ear patterns on poster board. Trace around and cut two each. Cut out buffalo face. Pin mane pattern to back of fur and cut it out.

2. Color front of horns with black and grey lines. Color front of ears brown. Color buffalo face to mane area brown with a black nose. Leave eye circles uncolored.

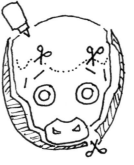

*Buffalo Headdress & Mask continued on page 68*

**Three Musical Instruments**

# Three Musical Instruments

## LAKOTA SIOUX TURTLE RATTLE

*Materials: Two pieces of poster board 12" x 12", scissors, glue, brown and yellow markers, 10 yellow feathers, one wide craft stick, stapler, turquoise, bright blue and white paint, regular brush, four ½" spacers, beans or something similar for the rattle sound. Pattern on page 71.*

1. After copying the pattern lay it on the two poster board pieces and trace around it. Cut out the double shapes and the single checkered stomach piece. Grid it and color in the brown and yellow squares.

2. Glue the double poster board edges leaving a 3" space on the stomach side. Cut ½" spacers (we used small pieces of ordinary sponge) and glue them in four different inside evenly spaced edges of the stomach hole. Now you have made a cavity where beans can rattle. Fill the cavity with beans, (or pebbles, dry corn, etc.).

3. Paint the turtle turquoise. Give it bright blue stripes (this was all patterned beads) Glue the craft stick in place and paint it. Glue the checkered middle piece in place. Glue the feathers on the ends of the turtle's extensions. Make two white eyes. Give the rattle a shake!

## ASSINIBOIN DONUT RATTLE

*Materials: Two 6" pieces of poster board, scissors, stapler, buckskin colored paint, sponge, one yard of hemp twine, one craft stick, 2" x 6" of black felt, two small feathers, paper painted buckskin strips, beans for the rattle, six small sponge spacers, masking tape, red marker or paint.*

1. Cut out two 6" circles. Find the center and cut out two 2½" holes. Glue the six small spacers on the bottom donut equal distances from one another (we used small sponge pieces). Glue the handle to the bottom circle.

2. Staple the outside donut edges together. Leave a 2"–3" gap. Masking tape the inner hole leaving a ½" edge of space. Push the beans from the outer gap trying to distribute them evenly around the shape (keep shaking it) until the rattle sounds right.

3. Mix the paint and sponge it onto both sides of the circle piece. Line the handle with black felt and then wrap with the twine inserting the paper strips and the feathers at the bottom as you wrap. Paint a red line around the rattle.

*Three Musical Instruments continued on page 70*

**Necklace & Breastplate**

# Necklace & Breastplate

## NECKLACE OR CHOKER

*Materials: 7 white straws (probably only flexible striped straws are available), white plastic mesh (found in craft stores in needle craft area) with 7 holes per inch, scissors, 30 colored beads, 55" of dental floss, 18" of narrow ribbon, ruler.*

1. Lay straws out and mark with pencil to get four sections each 1 3/4" from each straw. Cut on marks. This will make 28 sections, only 25 sections are needed.

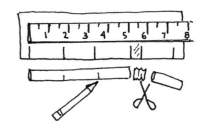

2. Cut six strips of mesh with nine holes in each strip. These are narrow strips, 1 3/8" long. Lay out the strips. Tie a three foot piece of floss to outside edge of hole 1 on strip one. Secure with several knots. Repeat the process working from left to right.

3. Thread floss through strip one, hole 1. Thread a bead, then a straw, then a bead. This sequence is exclusively for spaces between strip one and two. After strip two, thread a straw, then a bead, and strip three. Thread a straw, a bead, and strip four. Repeat to fifth and sixth strips. After sixth strip is in place you are ready to change direction.

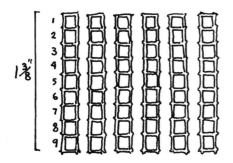
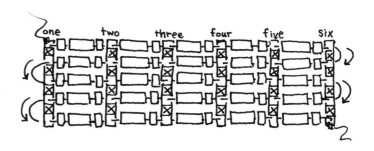

4. Skip a hole to properly space straws and beads. You will be threading holes 1,3,5,7 and 9 in each strip. Going from right to left through strip six, hole 3, thread bead, straw, strip five. Thread bead, straw, strip four, bead, straw, strip three; bead, straw, strip two. You are back between strip two and strip one. Thread bead, straw, bead, strip one.

5. It is time to change direction. Thread strip one, hole 5 with bead, straw, strip two. Next straw, bead, strip three, straw, bead strip four…strip five…strip six. At some point you will need to tie on more floss. Secure with several knots and continue, repeating your pattern. To end your necklace, secure with multiple knots. Cut ribbon in half. Attach one to each end of necklace and tie in bow at back of neck.

*Necklace & Breastplate continued on page 68*

Three Indian Dolls

# Three Indian Dolls

## AN ARAPAHO DOLL OF FELT

*Materials: Four 10" x 10" squares of beige felt, two light and two darker, natural colored yarn or string, a big-eyed needle, black fleece, glue, chalk, scissors, red, black, blue markers or acrylic paint, stuffing for doll. Pattern on page 75.*

1. Cut out the two light-beige felt pieces around the outline of the pattern. We sewed the pieces together with beige thread using the blanket stitch. To save time glue the felt pieces together and let dry overnight. Be sure to leave a 3"–4" gap between the legs for stuffing the doll.

2. Stuff the doll and sew up the leg gap. Lay the doll on the dress felt pieces. Trace the doll's form with chalk. Cut out the two dress pieces bigger than the doll. Try the pieces on the doll. If they fit, decorate the front of the dress with a yellow painted yoke, string fringes and red peaks above the felt fringe. Put colorful moccasins with paint or marker on the feet.

3. Paint or marker the nose, cheeks and eyes on the face. Prepare the braided hair by cutting three strips of fleece 12" long and ¼" wide. Braid the two ends and glue the middle onto the doll's head. Open for slipping over the head. When the glue has dried put the dress on the doll sewing or gluing the gap.

## A CROW DOLL OF FELT AND COTTON

*Materials: Two pieces of cotton the size of this page, pattern of doll, two pieces of red felt for the dress, white buttons, narrow colored ribbon for trim, white dots of paint (to resemble beads or elk teeth), stuffing, two yards of black yarn.*

Follow the instructions for the felt doll either gluing or sewing both the doll and the dress, after the dress has been decorated.

## A MANDAN DOLL OF PAPER

*Materials: Four pieces of paper 9" x 12", that have been washed with beige paint (the real doll is made of soft, treated animal skin), glue, stuffing, black yarn, blue felt for dress trim, red, yellow, black, white paint, scissors.*

Follow the instructions for the felt and fabric dolls except only use glue. Many museum doll samples do not have facial features.

*Three Indian Dolls continued on page 69*

**Three Shields**

# Three Shields

## CHEYENNE SHIELD WITH SYMBOLS

*Materials: Matte board in a 13" circle, sponge, buckskin colored paint, thin-tipped paint brush, pencil, black, turquoise, red, yellow, lavender paint and markers, paper feathers\*, hemp twine, glue, scissors, three replicated feathers.*

## COMMANCHE SHIELD WITH CENTER BLUE STAR

*Materials: Matte board in a 10" circle, sponge, red and black strips of fleece, yellow, blue, black, red, paint, thin-tipped paint brush, pencil, small natural feathers, four replicated feathers, scissors, glue.*

## PLAINS INDIAN SHIELD IN DIVIDED TRIANGLES

*Materials: Matte board in a 9" circle, sponge, buckskin paint color, black, red, blue, yellow, chartreuse paint, fine-tipped brush, pencil, glue, scissors, six replicated feathers, ten real feathers, hemp twine.*

## GENERAL INSTRUCTIONS FOR THE THREE SHIELDS

1. Design the shield in a circle before it is cut out of matte board. Use a circle template such as a plate, lid, etc. Draw the design onto the circle.

2. Mix the buckskin paint (beige, yellow, brown, white) and sponge it onto the shield circle. Let the paint dry. Paint over the drawn details with the brush and various paint colors. Let the paint dry.

3. Lay out the pre-made paper feathers on a protected surface. Glue the hemp twine strings (cut according to the feather decoration for each shield) to the bottom of the feathers. Glue on the real feathers when called for. Glue the free end of the twine to the back of the shield. Glue all other trim to the shield. Glue an 8" band of poster board on the back for holding the shield.

*\*See instructions for making paper feathers on page 63.*

*Three Shields continued on page 69*

**Cheyenne Horses Headgear**

# Cheyenne Horses Headgear

*Materials: White poster board 15" x 10", yellow or white poster board 15" x 8", paper cutter for easy cutting, yellow, red, black, and green paint, big bristle brushes, ruler, pencil, lids for circle, ribbons, natural feathers, brown stained or painted paper 8" x 16".*

1. The woven headpiece measures 15" at top and 10" at bottom. Measure the center of the white poster board and mark it. Measure horizontal pencil lines every ½" from top to bottom. Cut the lines with scissors with an inch border on all four sides remaining uncut. Cut the 1/2 inch yellow strips with a paper cutter. There should be 14 strips ½" x 15".

2. Weave the yellow strips (or white), which is the weft through the horizontal paper "warp". Push the warp strips to tighten the weave.

3. Paint the paper strip with light brown paint or stain with tea or coffee. When it has dried cut the fringe for a mane 3" deep.

4. After weaving the strips, divide the poster board into four equal sections. Pay attention to the half-way mark. Paint the piece red and yellow as in the picture. Paint any leftover poster board strips red, green and black, Mark eye holes 1½ inches from center. Trace a 2½" lid around two scraps of poster board. Cut out the center leaving two ½" rings. Paint it yellow and fill the hole with black paper glued in place. Glue each eye in place paying close attention to symmetry.

5. Measure top of headgear at 12" and the bottom at 8". Draw a connecting line on both sides and cut along the line to give the piece the tapering of a horse's head.

6. Glue feathers and ribbons in place on top and bottom. Glue painted strips above trim. Glue mane strips on each side. Place a weight on the newly glued parts of the piece as it dries. When it is dry, bend over a 6–8", (such as a coffee can) round object with the front facing up.

**In 1650 the first Indians (Comanche) traded with the Spaniards for horses. The Spanish ponies originated with the Moors (Arabians) and were ideal for the plains because they were wiry, stiff and hardy animals. The horse radically changed the Indian way of life. An 1860–1872 count estimated the following tribal ration of horses to Indians: Kiowa and Comache 3:1; Blackfeet and Crow 2:1; and Flathead and Nez Perce 11:1. Many horses were obtained from raids or by bartering along the trade routes. Horses could pull larger travois so tipis could be larger and more storage was possible. An Indian male's primary importance was as protector, hunter and provider. Much depended upon his wealth in horses. With more horses and better hunting, there was too much work for one wife, so men often took more wives.**

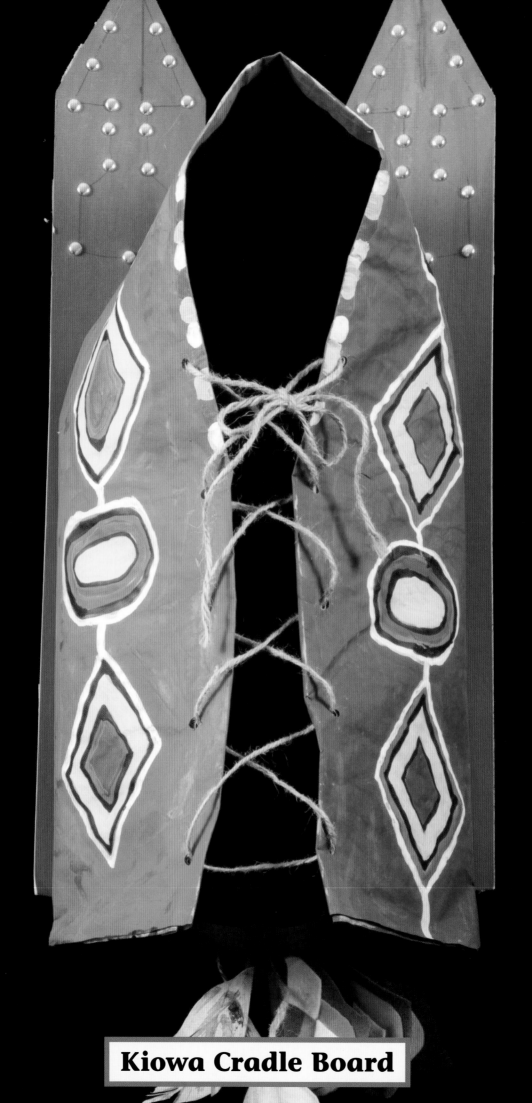

**Kiowa Cradle Board**

# Kiowa Cradle Board

*Materials: 12" x 24" matte board, paper cutter, 40 brass brads, school paper four thicknesses with the final strip measuring 10" x 40". A black paper strip 40" x 10". Glue, scissors, rough twine, stapler, acrylic or poster paint in red, blue, yellow, white, brown and black. Large and small brushes, pencil, 36" ruler, large nail, towel, hammer, hole punch.*

1. Cut matte board on a large paper cutter (use a box cutter if necessary). Measure and mark two long braces 22" x 3". Cut them tapering to a point at the top end. Cut two cross braces 11" x 3". Glue the cross braces 3" from the bottom and 5" from the top. After gluing in place put heavy weights on them overnight.

2. Cut diamond and oval templates from a folded newspaper as patterns. Cut and fold in four thicknesses your strip of school paper. Fold the length in half. The long strip when folded should be 21" to 24". Draw around the patterns onto the paper strip. Paint one end blue and the other red. Paint the brace brown.

3. After the paint has dried, make the holes for the brass brads. Cut an arrow shape 7" long that fits within the tapered ends. Pencil the arrow shape onto the matte board. Place one end of the brace face side up on a rolled-up towel. Hammer the nail, making holes 1" apart. Part the brad stem a little and insert it through the hole. Reach under and separate the stems. Repeat this on the other tapered end.

4. Paint the pencil patterns. Make the scalloped design on the edge. When the paint is dry lay the strip out and glue the long black paper strip about 1" from the edge. Put weights (such as books) on it as it dries. Punch holes for lacing 2"–3" apart, lining them up on both sides.

5. Fold 1"–2" of the back of the painted paper strip with edges facing inward. Lay the paper "buckskin" piece on the brace, curving the top and making sure the red/blue top is centered. Staple the folded edges to the brace. Cut the last black paper strip to fit the inside and glue in place. Place weights to keep the edges down while the glue is drying (we used large juice cans—something round). Lace the rough twine through the holes. Finally, add the beaded fringed bottom piece.

Traditionally, mothers placed their infants in baby carriers made of narrow wooden slats which projected above the baby's head. A buckskin bag for carrying the baby (often a beaded work of art) was fastened up the front. The back brace allowed the mother to hang the baby from a safe support while her hands were free to work. The baby could watch the mother as she cooked, tanned hides, gardened, or performed her other chores. If the camp moved, the cradle board was fastened to the saddle or the travois pole.

**Ownership Staff**

# Ownership Staff

*Materials: Stick or dowel piece 2–4 feet long and ½" wide, 10 colored feathers, 20 big-hole beads, 15 large and small paper feathers, colored narrow ribbon 10"–15" long, fringed black "school" paper 15" x 10" strips, ¼" of colored felt in several colors, paint or big-tipped markers in several colors, black raffia, bells (optional), personal framed pictures of visuals such as a portrait, sport, family, pet, favorite food, hobby, etc., glue, scissors, straws, hole punch, trim of any flashy kind.*

1. Prepare the personal visuals on colorful backgrounds and even colored frames. Make them interesting shapes too. Fold the black paper strip and cut into 1/4" strips leaving a 1" uncut top. Make the fake paper feathers* Mark the stick every five inches. Paint or color half of the 5" sections. Now everything in the materials section has been assembled and the staff will come together effectively.

2 Mount the personal picture at the top of the staff. Glue straw behind the photo. Wrap felt or raffia around stick over the attachments that extend from the photo. Glue four 1" strips of black paper behind picture. Stick bright feathers into straw tops. Continue down the stick wrapping felt strips, securing black paper fringe, ribbons, fake and real feathers. As each felt strip is wrapped glue each end tucking the feathers, etc. under the felt. Work down the stick.

3. Several inches from the bottom, end with paper strips and colored feathers. Tie the personal visuals to the ribbon ends.

**The Ownership Staff in the Plains Indian culture was personal, flamboyant, and decorative. The production involved hours of planning, gathering items, and then making the staff. Our staff is not strictly Indian but is inspired by the traditional staffs. They were made from a sapling 8–9 feet tall. The carved, painted staff was displayed in front of the tipi, wigwam or lodge and gave the camp a bright, vertical look. Other staffs were ceremonial lances used in parades and dances. Coup (coo) sticks were used by warriors to strike an enemy. It was considered a great honor to "count coup" in a battle and even better if the enemy was not wounded. A warrior could "count coup" with a bow, a quirt, or any stick at all but warriors carried a special coup stick.**

*\*Making paper feathers: Use any plain white paper. Draw a feather shape of any size (from 4" to 12"). Cut out the shapes. Brush or sponge paint with a diluted brown paint on both sides of the paper feathers. Let dry. Fold each feather down the middle. Give the feathers a mottled look with a big dry brush and contrasting colors such as black or white. Cut slanted fringe along each feather edge. For the staff glue a 4"–6" string to the feather base.*

# The Essential Buffalo

The Plains Indians relied on the buffalo for 90% of their needs.
Pictured are just a few of the items produced from the buffalo.

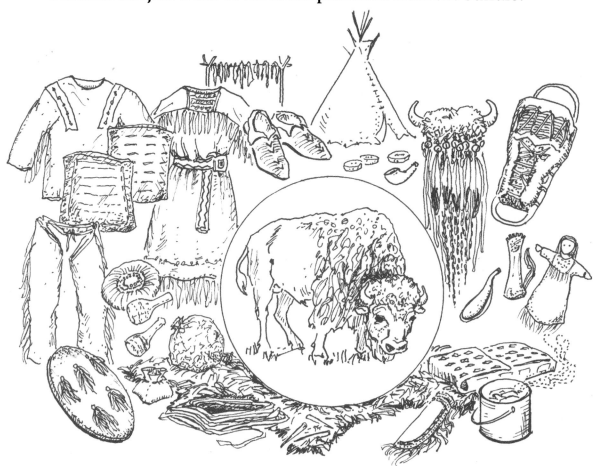

The Plains Indians were creative and effective in their hunting techniques: shooting the animal with a gun or bow and arrow, wearing animal hides as they crept close to a herd, and running stampeding buffalo off a cliff.

Women cleaned, scraped, tanned and dried the hides for use.

# Use of the Buffalo

**EDIBLE PARTS**
**FRESH**
meat
marrow
tongue
intestines
liver
other innards
blood

**EDIBLE PARTS**
**PRESERVED**
jerky
fat
marrow

**HIDE TANNED**
tipi covers
moccasin tops
leggings
dresses
breech clothes
robes
bedding
belts
caps
mittens
bags
pouches
dolls
trade items

**HIDE RAW**
containers
sheaths
moccasin soles
shields

rattles and drums
saddles and bridles
lariats
bull boats
masks
bindings
snowshoes
ornaments

**HORNS**
cups
spoons
ladles
fire carriers
powder flasks
toys
headdresses
rattles
buttons

**BONES**
knives
arrowheads
shovels
hoes
sled runners
saddle trees
war clubs
scrapers
awls
paint brushes
game counters
ceremonial objects
tool handles

**HAIR**
head dresses
padding and stuffing
ropes
halters
ornaments

**HOOVES & FEET**
glue
rattles

**TAIL**
medicine switch
fly brush
whips
ornaments

**BLADDER & STOMACH**
cooking vessels
water vessels
basins
pouches
buckets
cups

**SINEW (MUSCLE)**
thread
bow backings
bindings
bowstrings

**BRAIN**
hide tanning

**DRIED DUNG**
fuel
smoking

# Draw a Horse

## HOW INDIANS DREW THEIR HORSES

Plains Indians highly valued their horses, painting pictures of them on buffalo robes, shields, and tipis. They drew their horses in action—in races, on hunts, and in battles. Horses, like their riders, were often decorated in preparation for battle. The horse's head and neck could be streaked with red and yellow paint and decorated with feathers and streamers. The body could be painted with symbolic patterns such as stripes, circles and zigzag lines. Tails could be doubled in knots, tied short and hung with streamers.

Members of the war party at the top of the page have been painted in the style shown below them. Draw and decorate your own Indian horse using historic Plains Indian styles of drawing or decoration.

# Sign Language

The Great Plains was home to many different Indian groups who spoke different dialects and languages. A common sign language was used in trading, the making of treaties, and for other necessary communications between tribes.

By 1885 there were an estimated 110,000 sign-talking Indians among Plains tribes such as the Blackfeet, Cheyenne, Sioux and Arapaho.

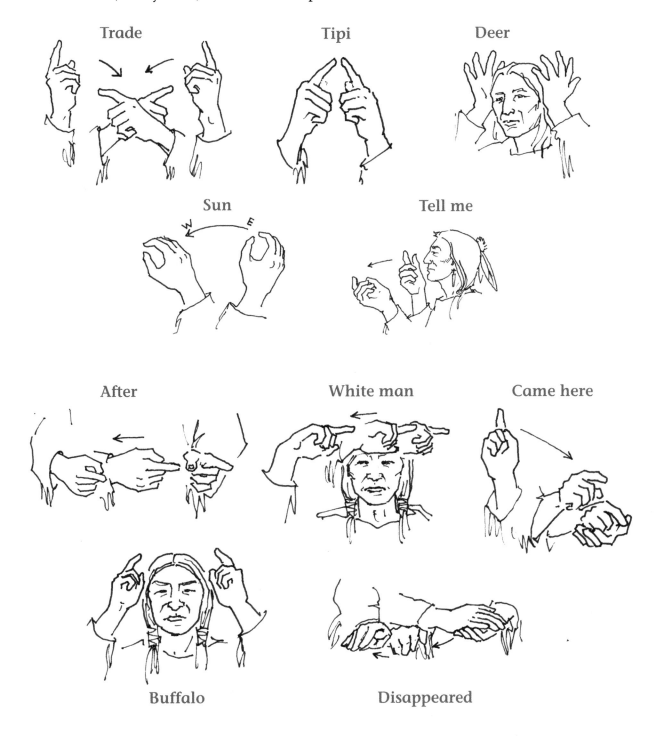

Trade          Tipi          Deer

Sun          Tell me

After          White man          Came here

Buffalo          Disappeared

# Sacagawea

*continued from page 11*

Sacagawea was a teenage Shoshone woman who, with her French Canadian husband Toussaint Charbonneau and their baby boy Jean-Baptiste (nicknamed "Pomp" by Clark), accompanied Lewis and Clark over thousands of wilderness miles to the Pacific and back.

Sacagawea had been kidnapped from the Shoshones at the age of 12 by Hidatsa warriors who carried her east to a Mandan village in North Dakota where Lewis and Clark met her. Because she spoke Shoshone and was familiar with western lands, she would be valuable to the expedition who needed Shoshone horses and information to successfully cross the western mountains.

Sacagawea traveled with the Corps from May 1805 to August 1806. She met with Shoshones, reuniting with her brother who helped provide necessary horses and guides through the Bitteroot Range. Because a woman and child traveled with the group, tribes did not consider them threatening. Sacagawea traveled by foot, in boats and by horseback over plains, rivers and mountains.

# Buffalo Headdress & Mask

*continued from page 49*

3. Glue buffalo face to plate so nose curves down over rounded edge. Cut away extra sides of plates. Cut slots for horns and ears. Insert 1/2" and tape inserts. Glue on buffalo mane. Cut out inner eye circles. Staple one end of headband to plate above ear. Size child's head and staple other side.

Because of the critical importance of the buffalo to the Plains Indians, huge ceremonies were held to lure and honor this essential animal. Pulsing drums and shaking rattles provided music while masks and other ceremonial items transformed dancers into fierce hunters and mighty buffalo.

# Necklace & Breastplate

*continued from page 53*

## THE BREASTPLATE

*This favored ornament for men and women is similar to the necklace but requires five times more material.*

1. Lay out straws and cut off at flex. Cut remaining straw into two 3/4" pieces, ending with 70 pieces. Cut four 7" mesh strips. Threading alternate holes, using 23 holes, giving the breastplate three sections.

2. Thread from left bead, straw in first section, bead, straw, bead in second section, straw, bead in third section. Complete by tying ribbon to left and right strips and hang from neck.

Plains Indians traded broadly for practical items like furs, food and horses. In addition, trading provided ornamental objects like seashells from the Pacific and Gulf of Mexico. Shells such as abalone, conch and dentalium were highly desirable. The long slender dentalium and hair pipes, and drilled shell and bone pieces were especially prized for ear ornaments, necklaces and breastplates.

# Veggie Prints

*continued from page 35*

**Here are more ideas for this technique: Print paper for a fan or wrapping paper.**

FAN

1. Fold paper in half. Draw two sides
of a triangle, curving one of the sides
as shown.

2. Cut out shape. Print designs on the flat
fan shape.

3. Mark lines for the fan pleats by using a ruler and scoring with a non-cutting tool.

4. Mark lines every inch on the curved part of the fan. Pleat accordion-style along the lines.

# Three Indian Dolls

*continued from page 55*

A doll began life as a simple shape cut from tanned animal skin and was stuffed with buffalo fur. If a child had long hair she might attach some of her own to the doll's head. She would decorate the skin dress with glass beads. Each tribe had its own style of dress which was reflected in the dress of the dolls.

Most dolls were the product of elderly women who made them as gifts for their granddaughters. Sewn with painstaking attention to detail, dolls and their accessories helped a girl learn about many skills in making household objects.

# Three Shields

*continued from page 57*

OTHER SHIELD DESIGNS

Shields were important protections in pre-horse days. They were seldom taken on the warpath, though they were always associated with the status of the pipe and the medicine bundle. Shields were heavy and cumbersome, and hampered the movements of the warriors in close combat. Eventually they would take the shield cover or a small replica into combat. It was the supernatural power of the shield which was represented in various forms that had been received as a vision.

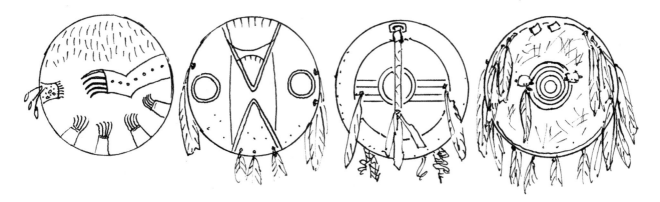

# Two Dwellings

*continued from page 17.*

## THE TIPI

1. Lay pattern on "aged" freezer paper. Trace around and cut out. Punch holes on dots.

2. Study the designs on Plains Indian tipis. Draw and color your tipi. Draw a 7" circle on the cardboard. Pencil six marks on the circle equal distances apart. Make holes on marks to hold the tipi sticks.

3. With the twist tie firmly tie three sticks about 2" from the ends. Add the other three sticks between the first three and tie these firmly. Drop glue in each hole and set stick into holes. Let dry. Lay tipi cover carefully over the cone-shaped sticks. Position holes and secure with toothpicks.

Earth lodges might be 40 feet in diameter and house 40–50 people. Tribes that grew crops and settled along rivers made these homes out of logs, willow branches, grass and sod. The entry faced east, and people watched celebrations from the roofs.

Tipis were strong, lightweight shelters of the nomadic Plains Indians. The outer covering was made of pieced buffalo hides and tall poles. Tipis were cool in summer, warm in winter and easily transported by dogs or horses as families followed the game and changing seasons.

Tipis were owned by women who helped one another stitch together 8–20 tanned hides for a single cover. They also helped each other set up and take down the tipi which could be 8–12 feet across and weigh up to 150 pounds. The entry to the tipi always faced east. Men painted the tipis with animals, scenes of battle and other tribal events and sacred symbols.

## Three Musical Instruments

*continued from page 51*

### WHITE MOUNTAIN APACHE VIOLIN AND BOW

*Materials: A cardboard tube 24" x 7", a flexible branch 24" long, 10 feet of strong (.021) monofilament, desert-colored paint, big bristled brush, fine tipped markers and paint for the tube designs, two small sponges to elevate the strings.*

1. Glue the two sponge pieces 4" from each end of the tube. After they have dried paint the branch and the tube with the chosen paint color.

Decorate the tube with the beautiful Apache designs with paint, marker, or a combination.

2. Notch the branch on each end and wrap the monofilament around one end, knotting it when the branch is bowed. Knot the opposite end. Cut two notches in front and back of the tube on both ends. Wrap the eight feet of filament around the tube lining up with the sponges and the notches for anchoring the strings. Knot them and cut the loose ends.

This piece was chosen for its beauty and ingenuity of design. It did not make music for us, but in other hands it might be a sound-producing instrument.

# Pattern Pages

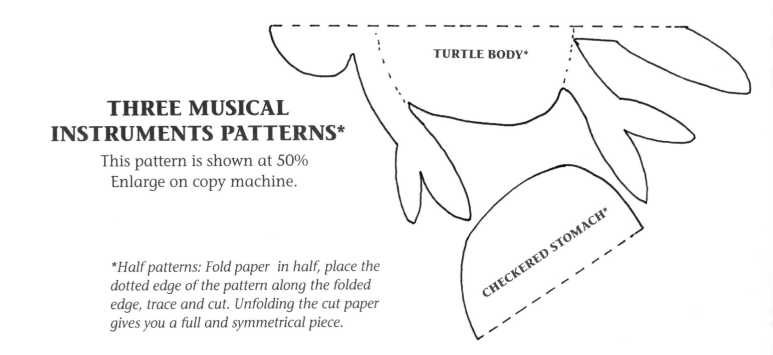

## THREE MUSICAL INSTRUMENTS PATTERNS*

This pattern is shown at 50%
Enlarge on copy machine.

*Half patterns: Fold paper in half, place the dotted edge of the pattern along the folded edge, trace and cut. Unfolding the cut paper gives you a full and symmetrical piece.*

**TURTLE BODY***

**CHECKERED STOMACH***

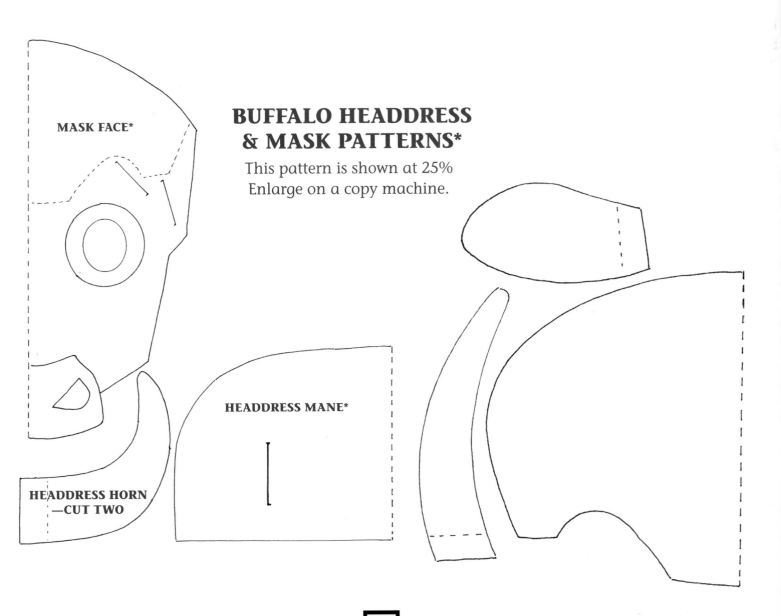

## BUFFALO HEADDRESS & MASK PATTERNS*

This pattern is shown at 25%
Enlarge on a copy machine.

**MASK FACE***

**HEADDRESS MANE***

**HEADDRESS HORN —CUT TWO**

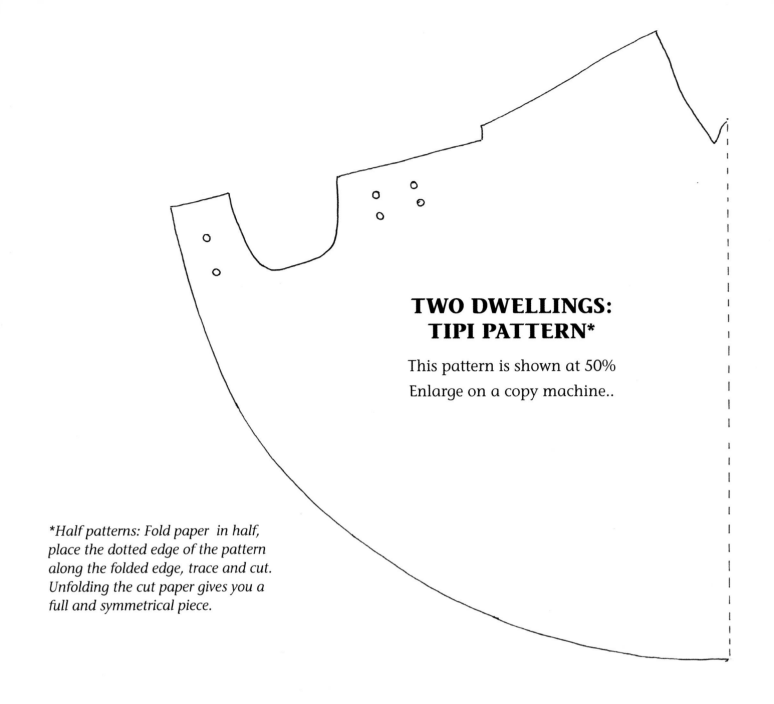

# TWO DWELLINGS:
# TIPI PATTERN*

This pattern is shown at 50%
Enlarge on a copy machine..

*Half patterns: Fold paper in half, place the dotted edge of the pattern along the folded edge, trace and cut. Unfolding the cut paper gives you a full and symmetrical piece.

# SACAGAWEA PATTERN

This pattern is shown at 75%
Enlarge on a copy machine.

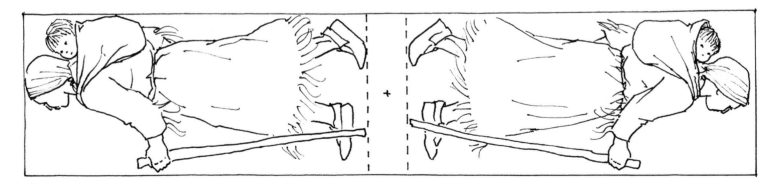

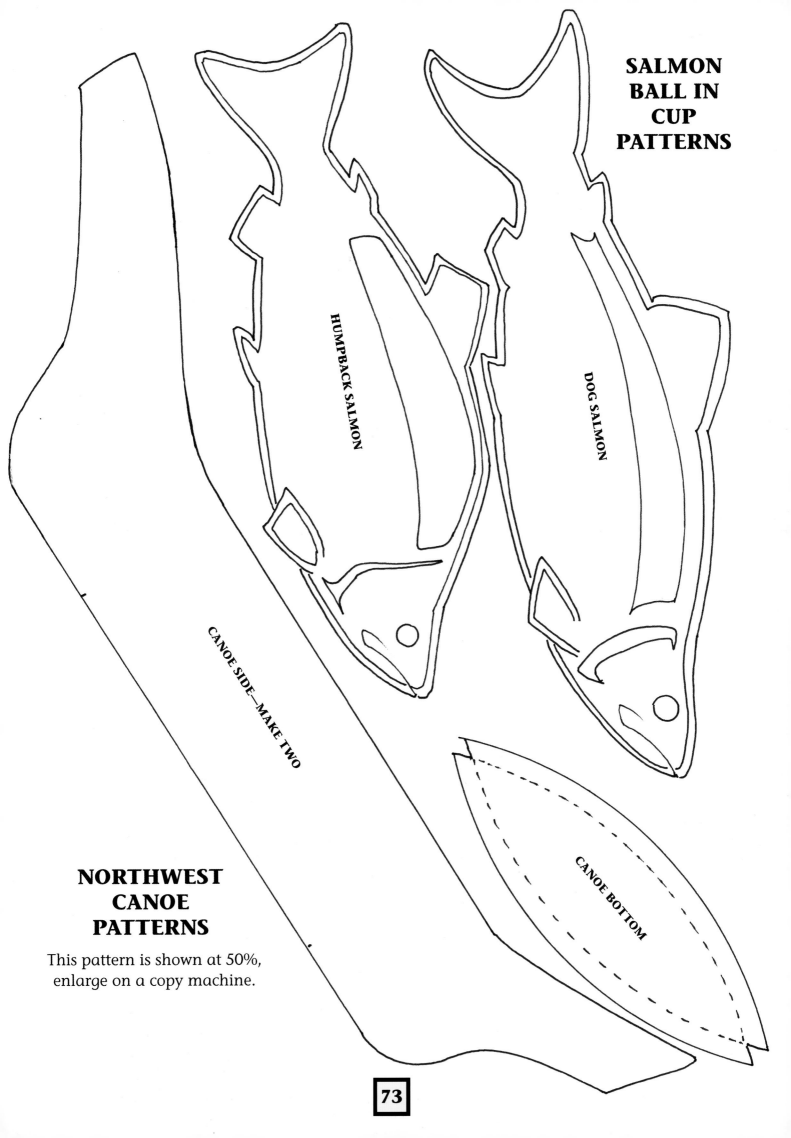

SALMON
BALL IN
CUP
PATTERNS

HUMPBACK SALMON

DOG SALMON

CANOE SIDE—MAKE TWO

CANOE BOTTOM

NORTHWEST
CANOE
PATTERNS

This pattern is shown at 50%,
enlarge on a copy machine.

73

# SLOTTED ANIMALS PATTERNS

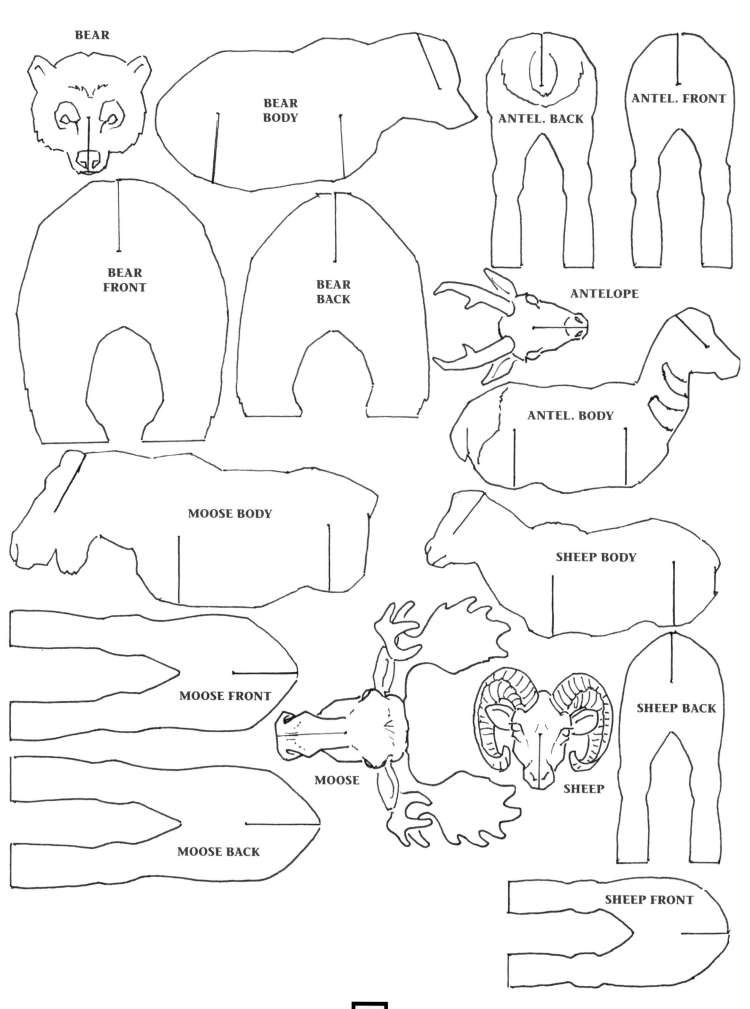

BEAR

BEAR BODY

ANTEL. BACK

ANTEL. FRONT

BEAR FRONT

BEAR BACK

ANTELOPE

ANTEL. BODY

MOOSE BODY

SHEEP BODY

MOOSE FRONT

MOOSE

SHEEP BACK

MOOSE BACK

SHEEP

SHEEP FRONT

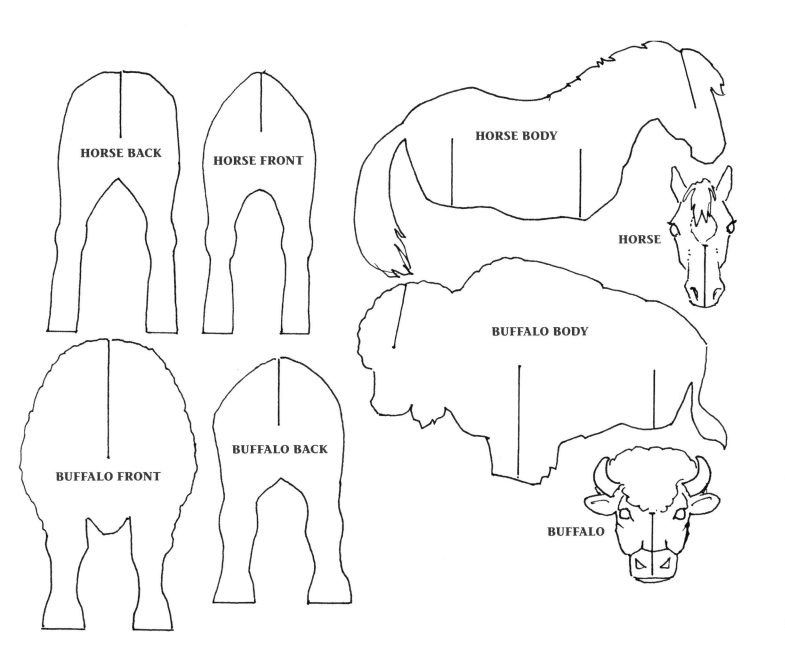

**HORSE BACK**

**HORSE FRONT**

**HORSE BODY**

**HORSE**

**BUFFALO FRONT**

**BUFFALO BACK**

**BUFFALO BODY**

**BUFFALO**

# THREE INDIAN DOLLS PATTERN*

This pattern is shown at 50%
Enlarge on a copy machine.

*Half patterns: Fold paper in half, place the dotted edge of the pattern along the folded edge, trace and cut. Unfolding the cut paper gives you a full and symmetrical piece.

# DESIGN MOTIFS

## NORTHWEST COAST INDIAN DESIGNS

## PLAINS INDIAN DESIGNS

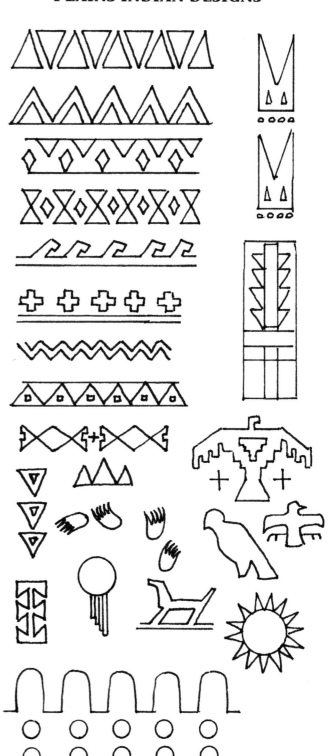

# Bibliography

## LEWIS AND CLARK SECTION:

Ambrose, Stephen E., *Lewis and Clark: Voyage of Discovery*, National Geographic Society, Washington, DC, 1998.

Blumberg, Rhoda, *The Incredible Journey of Lewis and Clark,* First Beech Tree Edition, NY, 1995.

Blumberg, Rhoda, *York's Adventures with Lewis and Clark,* Harper Collins Publishers, NY, 2004.

Copeland, Peter F., *The Lewis and Clark Expedition Coloring Book,* Dover Publications Inc., NY,1983.

Edwards, Judith, *The Great Expedition of Lewis and Clark,* by Private Reuben Field, Phoenix Color Coloration, Farrar Straus Giroux, NY, 2003.

Herbert, Janis, *Lewis and Clark for Kids,* Chicago Review Press, Chicago, 2000.

Isaacs, Sally Senzell, *The American Adventure: The Lewis and Clark Expedition,* Heinemann Library, Chicago, 2004.

Kozar, Richard, *Lewis and Clark, Explorers of the Louisiana Purchase,* Chelsea House Publishers, Philadelphia, 2000.

Morley, Jacqueline, *Across America: The Story of Lewis and Clark,* Franklin Watts, Danbury, CT,1998.

Roop, Peter and Connie, *Off the Map,* Walker and Company, Ontario, Canada, 1993.

Snyder, Gerald S., *In the Footsteps of Lewis and Clark,* National Geographic Society, Washington, DC, 1970.

## PIONEERS SECTION:

Allison, Linda, *The Sierra Club Summer Book,* San Fransisco: Sierra Club Books, 1997.

Daughters of Utah Pioneers, *An Enduring Legacy: Pioneer and Old Dolls,* Salt Lake City: National Society of Daughters of Utah Pioneers, 1993.

Daughters of Utah Pioneers, *The Pioneer Cookbook.* Utah Printing Company, Salt Lake City, 1991.

Daughters of Utah Pioneers, *Pioneer Memorial Museum: A Collection of Pioneer Memorabilia and Excerpts from Pioneer Journals,* Salt Lake City: National Society of Daughters of Utah Pioneers, 1983.

Daughters of Utah Pioneers, *Pioneer Tales to Tell,* Salt Lake City: Paragon Press, 1989.

Hamilton, Leslie, *Child's Play: 200 Instant Crafts and Activities for Preschoolers,* Crown Publishers, NY, 1989.

Klinkenborg, Verlyn, *"Come Booooooooss! Come Booooooss!: the story of the Oxen that pulled the covered wagons",* Smithsonian Magazine 24, September, 1993, pp. 81-91.

Paxman, Shirley, *Homespun,* Deseret Book Company, Salt Lake City, 1976.

Time-Life Books, *The Old West: The Pioneers,* Time-Life Publishers, 1974.

Wiseman, Ann, *Making Things: The Handbook of Creative Discovery*, Little Brown and Company, 1973.

*Bibliography continued on page 78*

# Bibliography

*continued from page 77*

## PLAINS INDIANS SECTION:

Ansary, Mir Tamim, *Plains Indians,* Heinemann Library, Chicago, 2000.

Berlo, Janet C. and Ruth B. Phillips, *Native North American Arts,* Oxford University Press, Oxford, NY,1998.

Bial, Raymond, *The Comanche,* Benchmark Books, Tarrytown, NY, 2000.

Bial, Raymond, *The Mandan,* Benchmark Books, Tarrytown, NY, 2003.

Bial, Raymond, *The Cheyenne,* Benchmark Books, Tarrytown, NY, 2001.

Englar, Mary, *The Great Plains Indians: Daily Life in the 1700s,* Capstone Press, Mankato, MN,2006.

Feest, Christian F., *Native Arts of North America,* Thames and Hudson Ltd., London, 1992.

Fradin, Dennis B., *The Pawnee,* Childrens Press, Chicago, 1988.

Ketchum, William C., Jr., *Native American Art,* Smithmark, 1997.

McLuhan, T. C., *Touch the Earth: A Self Portrait of Indian Existence,* Promontory Press, NY, 1991.

Remington, Gwen, *The Sioux,* Lucent Books, San Diego, CA, 2000.

Taylor, Colin F., Dr., *What Do We Know About The Plains Indians?* Peter Bedrick Books, NY, 1993.

Taylor, Colin F., Dr., *The Plains Indians,* Peter Bedrick Books, NY, 1994.

Terry, Michael Bad Hand, *Daily Life in a Plains Village,* 1968, Clarion Books, NY,1999.

Time-Life Books, *American Indians: Tribe of the Southern Plains,* NY, 1995.

Warnock, John and Marva, *Splendid Heritage: Perspectives on American Indian Art,* University of Utah Press, Salt Lake City, 2009.

The projects in the Pioneer section of this book originated in the 1996 publication of Hands-on Pioneers, co-authored by Yvonne Y. Merrill and her daughter, Emily Merrill Mortensen. The book was published by Deseret Book, Salt Lake City, UT.

# Index

*Index continued on page 80*

# Index

continued from page 79

**Hands-on Alaska**
(ISBN 0-9643177-3-7)
**Limited Availability**

**Hands-on America Vol. I**
(ISBN 0-9643177-6-1)

**Hands-on Rocky Mountains**
(ISBN 0-9643177-2-9)

**Hands-on Latin America**
(ISBN 0-9643177-1-0)

**Hands-on Ancient People**
**Vol. II** (ISBN 0-9643177-9-6)

**Hands-on Celebrations**
(ISBN 0-9643177-4-5)

**Hands-on Ancient People**
**Vol. I** (ISBN 0-9643177-8-8)

**Hands-on Africa**
(ISBN 0-9643177-7-X)

**Hands-on Asia**
(ISBN 0-9643177-5-3)

**Hands-on America Vol. II**
(ISBN 0-9778797-0-4)

### Yvonne Merrill's
## KITS PUBLISHING

### Consider these books for:
the library • teaching social studies •
art • ESL programs • museum
programs • community youth events
• home schooling

**Hands-on America Vol. III**
(ISBN 0-9778797-1-2)

## Hands-on ORDER FORM

SEND TO:_____

ADDRESS:_____

CITY:_____ STATE:_____ ZIP:_____

CONTACT NAME:_____ PHONE:_____

PO#_____ FAX:_____ EMAIL:_____

**New Book Hands-on America, Vol. III is $25.00.**
**All other books are still $20.00 each.** Handling fee - $3.00
*All books shipped media rate unless otherwise requested.*

Make checks payable to:

KITS PUBLISHING • 2359 E. Bryan Avenue • Salt Lake City, Utah 84108
phone: (801) 582-2517 • fax: (801) 582-2540
email: info@hands-on.com
Kits Publishing Website: www. hands-on.com
blogsite: www.handsonkits.blogspot.com

☐ ____ Hands-on Africa
☐ ____ Hands-on Alaska
☐ ____ Hands-on America Vol. I
☐ ____ Hands-on America Vol. II
☐ ____ Hands-on America Vol. III ($25)
☐ ____ Hands-on Ancient People Vol. I
☐ ____ Hands-on Ancient People Vol. II
☐ ____ Hands-on Asia
☐ ____ Hands-on Celebrations
☐ ____ Hands-on Latin America
☐ ____ Hands-on Rocky Mountains

____ **Total Quantity Ordered**
$3.00 **Handling**
____ **Shipping**
____ **Total Enclosed/ PO**